GCSE PE for OCR

Heinemann

Heinemann Educational Publishers
Halley Court, Jordan Hill, Oxford,
OX2 8EJ
Part of Harcourt Education

Heinemann is the registered
trademark of Harcourt Education
Limited.

Text © Frank Galligan and David
White 2001

First published in 2001

05 04
10 9 8 7 6

**British Library Cataloguing in
Publication Data**
A catalogue record for this book is
available from the British Library

ISBN 0 435 50629 3

Illustration: Hardlines Ltd, Park
Street, Charlbury, Oxford, OX7 3PS
Cover photos by Photodisc, except
the rugby players by Corbis
Printed and bound in the UK by
Bath Colourbooks

Tel: 01865 888058 www.heinemann.co.uk

Acknowledgements

Acknowledgements
The publishers would like to thank the following for permission to use
photos:
ActionPlus pp.16, 19 (bottom), 23, 29, 30, 31 (all), 33 (top), 35 (both), 38,
44, 47 (bottom), 50, 51, 52, 57, 62 (both), 64, 70, 75, 801 811 82, 87
(bottom), 90, 91, 94, 96, 106, 109 (right and centre), 110, 111, 121 (right),
125, 140, 146, 153; Gareth Boden pp.32, 33 (bottom), 48, 55 (bottom), 98,
101, 107, 117, 121 (left), 130, 134, 135, 137, 141; Corbis p.69 (and rugby
players in montage on cover); DOEA Scheme p. 56; Empics pp. 17, 22,
37, 42, 46, 54 (left and bottom), 55 (top), 58, 63, 66, 67, 73, 78, 87
(centre), 97, 109 (left), 114, 119, 122, 144, 147, 148, 150; Sally and
Richard Greenhill pp.36, 54 (centre), 126, 132, 133, 138; Peter Morris
p.92; Photo Library Wales p. 129; Popperfoto pp. 19 (top), 25, 34, 40, 41
(both), 45, 47 (top), 53, 59, 60, 77, 87 (top), 88, 93, 95, 116, 141; Science
Photo Library p.28.

The publishers would also like to thank Eric Singleton and Jay Surti for
their invaluable assistance and support during the writing of this book. A
special thanks to Trinity High School and Sixth Form Centre and students
for the photoshoot.

The publishers have made every effort to trace the copyright holders, but
if they have inadvertently overlooked any, they will be pleased to make the
necessary arrangements at the first opportunity.

Websites
Links to appropriate websites are given throughout the book. Although
these were up to date at the time of writing, it is essential for teachers to
preview these sites before using them with pupils. This will ensure that the
web address (URL) is still accurate and the content is suitable for your
needs.

We suggest that you bookmark useful sites and consider enabling pupils to
access them through the school intranet. We are bringing this to your
attention, as we are aware of legitimate sites being appropriated illegally by
people wanting to distribute unsuitable or offensive material. We strongly
advise you to purchase suitable screening software so that pupils are
protected from unsuitable sites and their material.

If you do find that the links given no longer work, or the content is
unsuitable, please let us know. Details of changes will be posted on our
website to correct this at the earliest opportunity

contents

About your course

This book has been written for the OCR GCSE Physical Education specifications.

There are three ways in which you can study for a GCSE in PE with the OCR exam board:

- GCSE in Physical Education
- GCSE in Physical Education (Games)
- GCSE (short course) in Physical Education (Games).

This book can be used for all three of these specifications. If you are doing the short course, however, you will not have to know about all the information in this book. Again, your teacher will guide you on what you need to know for your course.

All three of the OCR GCSE PE courses involve both coursework and preparation for a written paper. For your coursework, you will choose four different types of activities (two if you are doing the short course). Over your course, you will work on how well you can do these activities, and at the end of the course you will be assessed on your performance in each of your activities. You will also carry out an 'analysis of performance' task for one of your activities, which involves trying to improve either your own or someone else's performance. We will look at what you need to do in your coursework in more detail in section 4 of this book.

Depending on what your school offers, if you are doing the GCSE in Physical Education, you can choose from the following list of activity areas (each area contains lots of different types of activity, which your teacher can tell you about):

- Games activities
- Gymnastic activities
- Dance activities
- Athletics activities
- Outdoor adventurous activities
- Swimming activities
- Exercise activities.

Your four activities need to come from at least two of these different activity areas (e.g. football and cricket from Games, cross-country running and track and field athletics from Athletics). If you choose an activity from the Exercise activities area, you have to then choose your other three activities from at least two other activity areas. If you live in Northern Ireland, your four activities need to come from three activity areas.

If you are studying PE (Games) or the Games short course GCSE, you have three activity areas to choose from:

- Invasion games
- Net/wall games
- Striking/fielding/target games.

Again, your four activities, or two in the case of those of you who are following the short course, need to come from at least two different Games activity areas.

How the book is set out

This book is in four sections. The first three sections give you information for the written paper (Paper 1) of your GCSE course. This exam is on the theory of PE and Games – the reasons why our bodies work like they do, what sort of factors improve performance in sport and physical activity, about fitness and health and different ways to get fitter and more healthy, and about safety.

This book follows the same order as the specification for the full course GCSEs. Your teacher will tell you which parts are relevant to you if you are studying for the short course.

You will be tested on this information in the exam at the end of your course – so this book will be useful to help you prepare for that. It will be very useful for your coursework as well. It will help you improve how well you can do your activities by giving you 'background information' about what helps us improve performance in sport and physical activity, what helps us be more fit and healthy, and how we can avoid getting injured.

There is a glossary of key terms on page 158. Words included there appear in **bold** in the text.

Practise, practise, practise!

To do well in your course, you need to practise. You need to practise your skills in your activities so you can improve them, of course. But you should also practise applying your knowledge about your activities and your theory knowledge too. For example, when you are warming up for an activity, you could try to remember what joints of your skeleton you are using.

Try to apply your theory knowledge in your practical work

The skeleton and joints

What the skeleton does

The skeleton is the basic framework of the body. It has four major functions:

- **shape and support**
- **movement**
- **protection**
- **blood production.**

It is important to remember that the body has other systems that support and enhance these functions as well.

These four major functions have important consequences for physical activity.

Shape and support

Without its rigid skeleton, the body would have no framework to support itself on – the skeleton gives us our shape.

The skeleton also gives the body its size. Taller people have longer bones than short people and in some cases the sturdiness or weight of the skeleton will influence overall bodyweight. See pages 86–8 which explains how body composition is an important factor affecting participation and performance.

Movement

How does a skeleton made up of hard, rigid bones move? The reason we can move is because of the joints between bones. Movement occurs when the muscles that are attached to the bones on either side of a joint contract (shorten) and make the joint move. This movement is called **articulation**.

So it's not just the joints of the skeleton that are important in movement: the skeleton provides something for our muscles to attach to. Without this, muscles couldn't produce movement, which is crucial to performance in all kinds of sport and physical activity in general.

Different joints work in different ways, and movement is greater at some joints than at others (see pages 8–11). The greatest range of movement is at the shoulder, the elbow and the wrist in the upper body, and the hip, the knee and the ankle in the lower body.

A smaller but still very important amount of movement is found at other joints such as in the hands, the neck and the spine in the upper body, and in the feet in the lower body.

Protection

The skeleton also fulfils a very important role in protecting the vital soft tissue organs of the body. Most important are:

- the rib cage – protects the heart and lungs
- the pelvic girdle – protects the abdomen
- the spinal column – protects the spinal chord
- the skull – protects the brain.

Blood production

Blood is made in **bone marrow** – particularly in the marrow of the long bones of the body. Blood contains both red and white blood cells. The red blood cells carry oxygen to muscles, which they need in order to work. The white blood cells fight infection in the body. There is more about blood later in this book (see pages 28–9).

Types of bones

There are over 200 bones in the body, and over 100 joints. The diagram on this page shows the bones you need to know about for this course.

Bones are divided into three main types:

- *flat bones* – the scapula, the patella, the sternum, the pelvis and the ribs
- *irregular bones* – the vertebrae and the short bones of the hands and feet
- *long bones* – the bones of the arms and the legs, and the long bones in the hands and feet.

Flat bones and irregular bones are usually protective bones: the skull, the ribs, the pelvis and the ribs protect vital organs. Other flat and irregular bones are also protective – the patella is a flat bone protecting the knee joint, for example.

Long bones are the 'levers' of the body – where lots of movement happens. The arm contains three long bones: the humerus, the radius and the ulna. The leg has three long bones as well: the femur, the tibia and the fibula. We also have long bones in our hands and feet: the phalanges and metacarpals that make up our fingers, and the phalanges and metatarsals of our toes.

Tasks

❶ List the *four* functions of the skeleton.
❷ Describe how bones and muscles work together to produce movement.
❸ Give an example from any sport of how each of the four functions of the skeleton plays a part in physical activity.

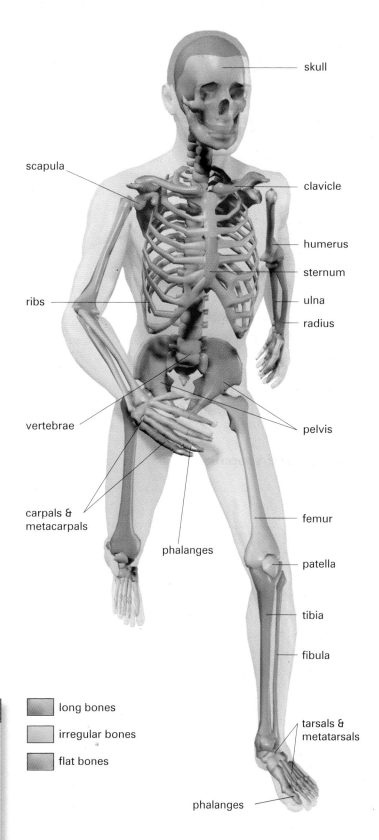

- long bones
- irregular bones
- flat bones

The major bones of the body

Joints and movement

There are many different types of joint in the body, including joints that do not move or move only slightly. We need to know about those involved in movement as these are vitally important factors affecting participation and performance.

Some joints support our whole body weight, so you can imagine that without something to reduce friction between moving bones and the pressure of one bone pressing on another, the bone ends would soon get damaged. This would severely affect our ability to move. So how do joints work to enable us to move freely?

Joint structure

Most moving joints are **synovial joints**. Synovial joints are enclosed inside a capsule filled with a lubricating fluid, called synovial fluid. This fluid greatly reduces the friction on the joint surfaces as they move against

each other. A membrane seals the synovial capsule so that the fluid doesn't leak out.

Cartilage

Joint surfaces are also covered by smooth, slippery **hyaline cartilage**. This cartilage aids in the production of synovial fluid.

Joints often also include another kind of cartilage, called white fibro-cartilage. While hyaline cartilage is smooth and hard in order to help free movement, fibro-cartilage is tough and elastic. It acts as a shock absorber, providing vital cushioning against impacts. Synovial joints like the knee contain fibro-cartilage to cushion the joint against the impact of walking, running and jumping.

Ligaments and tendons

Moving joints are held together by **ligaments** and **tendons**. Ligaments are very strong elastic fibres that keep joints intact, even under pressure. All the major joints of the body rely on a combination of ligaments and tendons for stability.

Tendons attach muscles to bones, and we will be looking at them in more detail on page 18. Both ligaments and tendons can be strained or torn as a result of violent movement.

Types of movement

Different kinds of joints allow different amounts of movement. Because movement is so important in sport and physical activity, we have special terms to describe these different kinds of movement:

- **flexion**
- **extension**
- **rotation**
- **abduction**
- **adduction**.

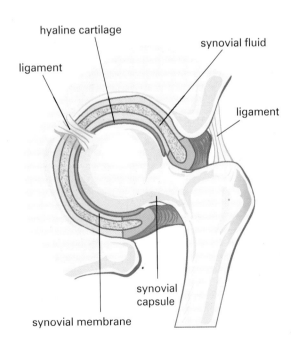

The hip joint is a synovial joint

Labels: hyaline cartilage, synovial fluid, ligament, ligament, synovial capsule, synovial membrane

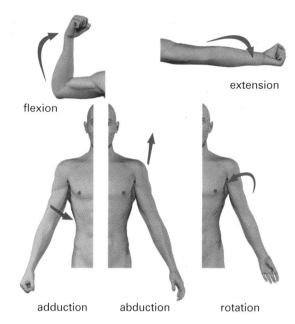

flexion

extension

adduction · abduction · rotation

Different types of movement

Flexion

Flexion is the bending of a joint. For example, flexion occurs at the knee as the foot is drawn back to kick a ball.

Extension

Extension is the straightening of a limb at a joint. For example, in putting the shot the elbow is straightened during release.

Rotation

Rotation is the 'swiveling' of a joint, for example moving the head from side to side.

Abduction and adduction

If there was a piece of string going through your body, from the top of your head straight down to the ground, it would mark the central axis of your body.

Abduction involves moving a limb or limbs *away from* the central axis of the body. *Adduction* is the opposite of abduction: moving a limb or limbs back *towards* the central axis of the body.

Types of joint

The types of joints that are particularly important for physical activity and sport are:

- **ball and socket joint**
- **hinge joint**
- **gliding joint**
- **pivot joint.**

Ball and socket joints

Of all the joints in the body, **ball and socket** joints allow the greatest range of movement. In this type of joint, one end of a bone is shaped like a ball, and it fits into a hollow socket at the end of another bone. This allows the joint to move up and down, from side to side and around. The joint is held together by ligaments and tendons, which give the joint stability. It is also a synovial joint, contained inside a capsule of synovial fluid and with hyaline cartilage on the two surfaces of the joint.

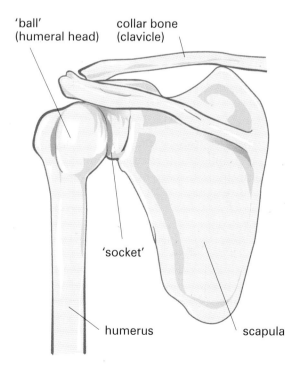

'ball' (humeral head) · collar bone (clavicle) · 'socket' · humerus · scapula

The shoulder joint is a ball and socket joint

The two main ball and socket joints are at the shoulder and at the hip. Move your whole arm around in different directions and you'll see just how great a range of movement this joint allows.

The shoulder joint allows the greatest range of movement: flexion, extension, abduction, adduction, and rotation. Bowling a cricket ball, for example, involves rotating the shoulder forward through a huge arc of movement. The hip joint allows a slightly smaller range. Both are vital joints for human movement, and are very strong.

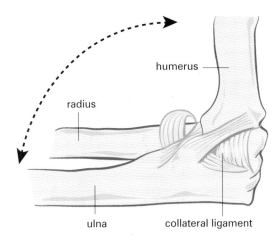

A hinge joint: flexion and extension at the elbow

Hinge joints

Hinge joints allow extensive flexion and extension (bending and straightening of the joint), but only a very small amount of rotation. The main hinge joints are the knee and the elbow.

In this type of joint, there is no socket for the ends of the bones to fit together in. Instead, the two bone ends have smooth hyaline surfaces that are shaped to move against each other, backwards and forwards, with the minimum of friction. Strong ligaments stop the bones from sliding off to one side or the other. So this joint works just like a door hinge.

Every time you bend your elbow or your knee, you are using a hinge joint. Squats are a good example of the knee joint in action, while curls are an example of the elbow acting as a hinge joint.

Like ball and socket joints, hinge joints are vital for movement and greatly affect participation and performance in sport – running, jumping and throwing all involve hinge joints. However, they have a more limited range of movement than the ball and socket as they can rotate only very slightly. This limited rotation can cause serious sporting injuries, especially at the knee as it has to support the weight of the body.

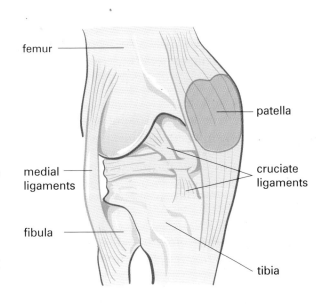

The knee joint: bound together by strong ligaments

The knee joint is, in effect, one bone, the tibia, balanced on top of another, the fibula, and held in place by ligaments. Strong twisting or turning of the joint puts great pressure on the ligaments holding the tibia and fibula together, and can damage them. This happens most often in sports involving physical contact or twists and turns, such as rugby or football tackles.

The knee joint is, the largest and most complex joint in the body. It is a synovial joint that also contains discs of white fibro-

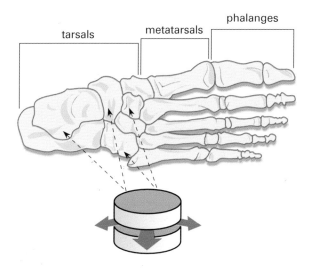

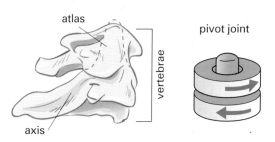

The pivot joint between the axis and atlas bones at the top of the spine

Gliding joints between the bones of the foot

cartilage to absorb shocks. Damage to this joint can badly affect performance and participation, sometimes even ending professional careers.

Gliding joints

Gliding joints allow flexion and extension through a slight gliding motion between the ends of the small bones of the hands and feet. These small bones can move over one another to increase the flexibility of the hands and the feet. Strong ligaments link them together and stop them from moving too far.

Pivot joints

Pivot joints allow only rotation. As the diagram at the top right of this page shows, a pivot joint works by the end of one bone having a 'peg' that fits into a 'ring' formed by the other bone.

There is a pivot joint at the top of the spinal column, between the axis and atlas bones of the neck. This joint allows us to turn, raise and lower our heads – crucial in controlling balance and maintaining awareness.

Joints and performance

Healthy and efficient joints are of paramount importance for performance in sport and physical activity. We have seen how joints are constructed in order to minimise friction and maximise free movement in the range the joint permits.

Because of this, it is very important to keep your joints as healthy as possible. **Flexibility** exercises can maintain a good range of movement, or even increase the range of movement joints allow. However, do not overstretch as this can damage ligaments and muscle tendons. Ligaments and tendons can also be strained or torn from violent movement and you should not undertake any activity without a full and correct warm-up procedure first. If you do injure a joint, then it should be allowed to heal properly, or you may face more permanent problems in later life.

Tasks

❶ Explain how and why a synovial capsule protects synovial joints.
❷ Describe, using the correct terminology, the movements at the elbow and knee joints during a basketball free throw.
❸ Select *one* movement from each of three activities of your choice and describe, using the correct terminology, the movements involved at specific joints.

Muscles

The structure and function of muscle

There are three types of muscle in the body:

- **involuntary muscle**
- **cardiac muscle**
- **voluntary or skeletal muscle.**

Involuntary muscle (also known as smooth muscle) is found in the body's internal organs. It is called involuntary as it is not under our conscious control.

Cardiac muscle is found only in the heart. It is also involuntary (we can't control it) and it never stops working until we die. It pumps blood from the heart around the body.

Voluntary or **skeletal muscle** (also known as 'striped' or 'striated' muscle) is under our conscious control and it is the type of muscle that makes us move.

How muscles work

Voluntary muscles produce movement by contracting and relaxing. They get shorter when they contract and longer when they relax again. All voluntary muscles are attached by tendons to bones (hence their other name: *skeletal* muscles).

The points of attachment by tendons to the bones are called origins and insertions. The origin does not move when the muscle contracts, while the insertion is the point which is moved when the muscle contracts. Some muscles, such as the biceps and triceps, have more than one attachment at one end and this is often an indication of their strength.

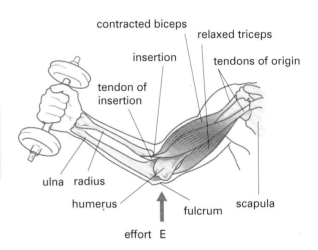

Contraction of the biceps bends the elbow with the triceps relaxed

Muscular contractions shorten muscles so that the muscle tendon at the point of insertion is pulled towards the point of origin. This creates the movement that allows us to walk, run and jump so it is central to all sporting and physical activity.

Movement at a joint is produced by muscles working together in pairs. When one muscle contracts on one side of a joint, a muscle on the other side of the joint relaxes. Muscles that work in this way are called **antagonistic pairs**. The muscle that contracts to produce a movement is called the **prime mover**. Other muscles sometimes assist the prime mover by contracting at the same time – these are known as **synergists**. They are 'helper' muscles.

An example of an antagonistic pair of muscles is found in the arm. Flexion of the hinge joint of the elbow is produced by the contraction of the biceps muscle and the relaxation of the triceps muscle. Extension of the joint happens when the triceps contracts and the biceps relaxes. We will look at more examples later.

Muscles for endurance and power

There are two types of muscle fibre present in voluntary muscle, each of which performs at its best under different conditions:

- **fast-twitch fibres**
- **slow-twitch fibres.**

Their names tell you about the way each type of fibre works. Fast-twitch fibres contract far more quickly and strongly than slow-twitch fibres. They are used most where short but powerful bursts of activity are required. Slow-twitch fibres contract far less violently but function for much longer periods of time. So:

- fast-twitch fibres are for short-term power and strength activities
- slow-twitch fibres are for longer-term endurance activities.

The ability of both types of muscle to do their work depends on the capacity of the circulatory and respiratory systems to deliver sufficient oxygen to them as it is needed. No muscles can function effectively without an efficient supply of oxygen (see page 20).

Fast-twitch muscle fibres burn up their supply of oxygen very quickly, usually within ten seconds or so. They then have to use an inefficient, short-term source of energy taken from the body's store of carbohydrates until more oxygen arrives. This is called **anaerobic** exercise.

Slow-twitch fibres work at a much slower rate and are able to replace their oxygen supply while they are still working. This allows them to work for much longer periods of time. This is known as **aerobic** exercise.

- anaerobic – working without oxygen
- aerobic – working with oxygen.

Fast-twitch or slow-twitch?

We cannot alter the distribution of muscle fibres in our bodies through training, however hard we try. This is determined by heredity.

A sprinter might have a distribution of 70 per cent fast-twitch fibres and 30 per cent slow-twitch fibres in their voluntary muscle, while a marathon runner might have almost the opposite proportions. Most of us have no idea what distribution of fast to slow fibres we have. However, those who are good at sprinting and power events are likely to have a higher proportion of fast-twitch fibres in their leg and shoulder muscles. The test to discover this precise distribution can only be done under specialised medical supervision.

Whether we use the aerobic energy of the slow-twitch fibres or the anaerobic energy of the fast-twitch fibres depends on the activity. Throwing the javelin, for example, takes just a few seconds of explosive, anaerobic power, while a cross-country run has to depend on the longer-lasting (but lower power) aerobic system.

Some activities require a combination of short bursts of all-out effort intermingled with periods of less frantic but sustained activity. Most team games are like this and so training programmes for games should contain elements to develop both aerobic and anaerobic fitness (see page 74).

Tasks

1. Describe the *three* types of muscle found in the body.
2. What is the difference between the origin of a muscle and its insertion?
3. Explain the terms *prime mover*, *antagonist* and *synergist*.

Muscles and performance

Voluntary muscles become stronger and more flexible the more they are exercised. When exercising or training stops, due to injury or for some other reason, muscles begin to lose the strength and mass that was gradually built up during regular activity. This is known as atrophy, or wasting of the muscles.

Improving muscle strength, flexibility and endurance will have obvious benefits for performance. Different activities rely on different muscles and different muscular requirements. One purpose of training is to develop and maintain muscular strength, flexibility and endurance in a way that is appropriate for the intended activity.

The major muscle groups

There are many different muscles and muscle groups in the body. You need to know about the following for your course. Look at the diagrams on this and the next pages for their position in the body.

- deltoids
- trapezius
- pectorals
- biceps
- triceps
- latissimus dorsi
- abdominals
- gluteals
- quadriceps
- hamstrings
- gastrocnemius.

It is important for you to know about the part these different muscles play in movement and performance. You also need to know how training and activity can make them stronger and more efficient.

The composition of all major muscle groups is affected by training and/or exercise. The specific nature of these changes – such as the building of muscle bulk – will depend upon the nature of any such activity.

Deltoids

The deltoid muscles lie to the front and rear of the shoulder. They provide additional protection and stability to the shoulder joint and assist in raising the upper arm.

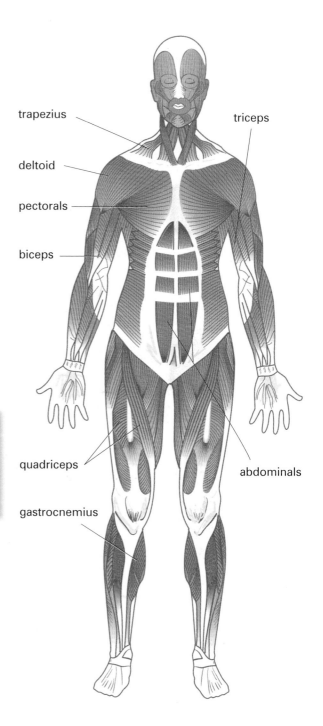

Major muscle groups: front view

The deltoid muscles become significantly pronounced in those performers who engage in sports involving the arms and shoulders.

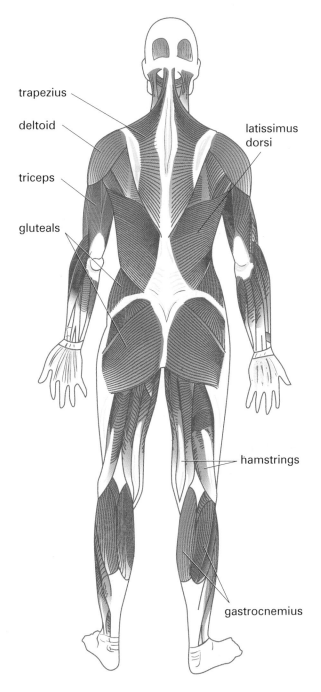

Major muscle groups: back view

trapezius

deltoid

triceps

gluteals

latissimus dorsi

hamstrings

gastrocnemius

Trapezius

The trapezius muscle assists in raising and lowering the head, shrugging the shoulders and the adduction of the scapular (shoulder blade) when reaching forward with the arms.

These muscles are often particularly pronounced in rugby forwards: rugby scrums require trapezius strength.

Pectorals

The pectoral muscles are situated across the front of the chest and have several insertions rather than just one. The pectorals assist in lifting or raising the arms above the head and in outward movement (adduction) of the upper arm.

Participation in activities involving considerable use of the arms and shoulders produces highly defined pectoral muscles. The extensive use of the arms and shoulder in swimming means that many such performers tend to develop strong pectorals.

Biceps

The biceps run along the front of the upper arm. These muscles have two origins ('bi' is the Latin for 'two'). Their main function is to bend the arm at the elbow joint and to act as antagonists to the triceps muscle when the arm is straightened. 'Athletic throwers', weightlifters and boxers have pronounced biceps because of their prominant use in those activities.

Triceps

The triceps muscles are found at the rear of the upper arm and assist in the straightening of the arms at the elbow such as in performing a press-up or putting the shot. The triceps and biceps together perform a similar role to the hamstrings and quadriceps in the thigh. The triceps has three origins ('tri' is Latin for 'three').

The biceps and triceps play a significant role in any activity involving a straightening of the arm at the elbow joint. This is clearly apparent in activities such as the shot putt or in the final lifting of a weight overhead in competition or training.

The elbow is bent by the contraction of the biceps muscle and the stretching of the triceps. The biceps and triceps muscles work as an antagonistic pair, so that to straighten the elbow they work in the opposite way: the triceps muscle contracts whilst the biceps relaxes or stretches. Flexion and extension of the elbow joint occurs in many throwing and serving actions in sport and during press-ups or curls with weights.

Latissimus dorsi

This large, sheet-like muscle has its origins along the middle and lower spine and its insertion in the upper arm. It is often referred to as a 'pulling muscle' and would be used, for example, in pulling on a rope or in climbing. When relaxed it allows the raising (adduction) or elevation of the arm away from the body and assists in pulling the elbow towards the rear of the line of the upper body. This muscle is much used by swimmers.

The latissimus dorsi muscles are particularly pronounced in many performers and produce the inverted triangle shape of the upper body associated with what is often referred to as an 'athletic physique'.

Abdominals

A large groups of muscles found at the front of the abdomen. The abdominal muscles assist in the action of breathing and in supporting the muscles of the spine in bending and lifting actions. These muscles play a major role in activities such as sit-ups and leg-raisers.

This group of muscles also plays a critical role in the prevention of back injuries. The spine runs down the back and the ribs provide support to the upper back. Between the rib cage and the pelvis, though, there is no equivalent to the ribs. Strong abdominal muscles are therefore particularly effective in supporting the front of the trunk and in minimising injuries, which may be caused by poor posture.

Gluteals

This is a collective term for the muscle group found in the buttocks. These powerful muscles assist in straightening the legs and trunk at the hip and are particularly important in sprinting, jumping and pushing actions.

The development of the gluteal muscles is quite different in a performer who engages in endurance activities as opposed to out and out power production. Muscular development in all muscle groups is far less pronounced where endurance activities are undertaken than is the case in activities where power optimisation is essential.

Abdominals play a major role in sit-ups

Quadriceps

This is another collective term. The quadriceps muscle group is made up of four separate muscles found at the front of the thigh. ('Quad' is Latin for 'four'.)

The quadriceps are the 'power muscles' at the front of the thigh and are significant in all activities involving straightening of the leg at the knee joint. As with the biceps and triceps of the upper arm, the quadriceps muscles work in opposition to the hamstrings (see below). Each group of muscles stretches or flexes in opposition to its antagonistic group as the knee joint is bent or straightened.

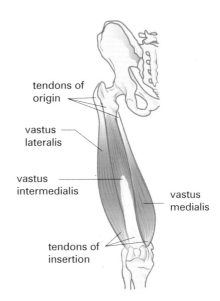

The quadriceps muscle group

Hamstrings

This group of muscles is often referred to as the 'leg biceps' because their role is similar to the biceps of the arms. As with the quadriceps, the three muscles of the hamstrings act as one. They assist in bending the legs at the knee joint in the same way that the biceps assist in bending the arms at the elbow.

The quadriceps are normally not as strong as the hamstring muscles at the back of the thigh and this imbalance is often the cause of hamstring injuries – particularly in soccer. In kicking a football, the foot is drawn through very quickly and the quadriceps muscles at the front of the thigh contract very strongly to straighten the leg at the knee joint. To allow this to happen the hamstring muscles must be relaxed and sufficiently supple to allow them to be stretched during the kick and the follow-through afterwards.

Injuries to the hamstring muscles are common in footballers, who often spend much time building up their quadriceps muscles and neglect the flexibility of their hamstrings. The force with which the ball is kicked often causes hamstring muscles to over-stretch. This results in muscle pulls, tears or damage to the tendons that attach the muscles to the bones.

The follow-through to any kick such as that shown in the illustration below places considerable strain on the hamstring muscles and flexibility/suppleness must be addressed in training and preparation.

Hamstrings, tendons and ligaments are stretched violently in this movement

Collectively, the quadriceps and hamstring muscles must carry the weight of the performer's body in addition to fulfilling their role in the performance of specific activities.

Gastrocnemius

The gastrocnemius is the calf muscle, and it is situated at the rear of the lower leg. It has two heads, which originate on either side of the knee. It unites with the soleus muscle to form the Achilles tendon, which has its insertion at the heel. This muscle assists in very powerful flexion at the ankle joint.

The gastrocnemius is more likely to be pronounced in those performers who undertake activities involving explosive flexing of the ankle joint.

The picture at the top of this page shows the movement of the heel and ankle joint at the point of take-off in the high jump or long jump event. As the heel strikes the ground the gastrocnemius is relaxed, allowing it to stretch whilst the muscles of the shin contract.

In the second of the two drawings above, the position is reversed, with the gastrocnemuis muscle contracting violently as the ball of the foot and then the toes push against the ground at the point of take-off.

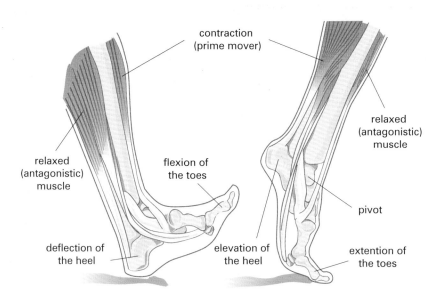

Antagonistic pairs in action: the long jump/high jump take-off

The work of tendons in movement

Tendons are the means by which muscles are attached to bones. They must be strong enough to work under heavy loads and also to resist the violent muscular contractions involved in sporting skills such as throwing the javelin or cricket ball. As a muscle contracts it is the tendons at each end that take the strain. The **tendon of origin** resists the pull of the muscle whilst the **tendon of insertion** exerts the pull on the bone to which it is attached. This in turn causes the joint to bend or straighten in the required manner.

The importance of the role of muscle tendons in sporting movement cannot therefore be underestimated. This type of connective tissue has a less efficient blood supply than skeletal muscle. A proper warm-up activity will stimulate blood flow to the tendons and this will reduce the chance of them being damaged by activity.

Training and exercise:

Its effect on muscle composition and efficiency

Skeletal muscle responds to training and exercise (or lack of it) in two distinct ways. Any prolonged period of inactivity causes muscle wastage (atrophy) whereas regular training and exercise contributes to greater muscle development (hypertrophy).

Muscles adapt very well to the workload they are required to perform and this is why some athletes develop muscle bulk whilst others do not. Where heavy workloads are involved, new muscle fibres are generated (muscle bulk) until specific groups of muscles become large enough and strong enough to perform the tasks they are asked to do.

In endurance activities where bulk is of no advantage, muscles adapt to training by utilizing energy much more efficiently in order to delay the onset of fatigue. Generally, muscles will not become any more bulky than they need to be.

The sprinter needs power and big, powerful muscles assist in this respect. A marathon runner needs to carry as little muscle bulk as possible in order to minimise both body weight and workload.

The sprinter's muscles are able to maximise stored energy in short bursts of all-out activity, whereas the distance runner's muscles utilise energy much more efficiently and for a much longer periods. Although 'fast-twitch' and 'slow twitch' muscle fibres (see page 13) can become more efficient through training, their distribution in the body cannot be altered.

Different activities rely on different muscles and different muscular requirements

Tasks

1. Which of the two athletes in the photos on this page would gain most by having a high level of fast-twitch muscle fibres?
2. Describe the differences in any weight training programme that might be undertaken by either of these two athletes.
3. Identify a specific muscle group that is important in any of your own practical activities. State whether you feel you need to increase power or stamina and outline how you might achieve this.

The circulatory and respiratory systems

Getting oxygen to the muscles

Our **circulatory system** is made up of the heart and the blood vessels that carry blood around the body. Blood carries nutrients to our organs, tissues and muscles, and takes away waste products. One of the most important nutrients blood carries is oxygen. Our muscles need oxygen to work so the efficiency of the circulatory system is a vital factor affecting performance.

The heart pumps blood around the body through a series of blood vessels called arteries and veins. Some of these blood vessels are quite large but become much smaller as they reach the body's extremities, such as our fingers and toes. Smaller arteries are known as arterioles and smaller veins are called venules. The smallest blood vessels of all are known as capilliaries.

Blood being pumped *away from* the heart flows through arteries and blood *returning to* the heart does so through veins.

The blood picks up oxygen at the lungs and then goes straight to the heart, which pumps it around the rest of the body, delivering oxygen as it goes. This means that by the time the blood gets back to the heart again, it has run out of oxygen. The heart pumps it back to the lungs where it picks up more oxygen, and the whole process begins again.

On the right is a picture of the heart. You don't need to know what all the parts are called for your exam, but it will be useful to know that the left side of the heart is the part

that pumps **oxygenated** (oxygen rich) blood around the body. The right side of the heart receives **deoxygenated** (oxygen poor) blood that has been round the body, and pumps it back to the lungs again.

The body's needs

It is important to understand that both the circulatory system and the **respiratory system** must work together in order for this to happen.

Every cell in our body needs oxygen and nutrients in order to produce energy. Cells

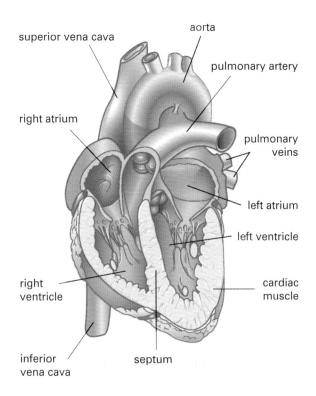

A section through the heart showing the four main chambers and blood vessels

use oxygen to break down the nutrients we get from the food we eat to release energy. As they do so, they produce waste products. These have to be removed or they would eventually stop the cells from working.

The respiratory and circulatory systems are responsible for delivering oxygen and food to all the cells of the body. The respiratory system brings the oxygen into the body and releases much of the waste product produced by respiration (the process of getting energy from food) out of the body.

Oxygen comes into the body from breathing in: air travels down into the lungs and from the lungs into the bloodstream. The blood delivers the oxygen to the cells, picks up the waste products and takes them to the organs in the body that dispose of them. One very important waste product produced by respiration is carbon dioxide. The blood carries this back to lungs, which release it out of the body again as we breathe out. We will look at the details of how this happens on page 26.

An efficient respiratory system ensures that the maximum amount of oxygen reaches the lungs and gets into the bloodstream. An efficient circulatory system ensures that this maximum amount of oxygen then gets pumped to the muscles and other organs, allowing them to work effectively. The better these two systems work, the better performance and participation in sport and physical activity are likely to be.

Our respiratory and circulatory systems have limits in terms of the amount of oxygen and blood that can be pumped around the body. These limits vary from one individual to another. Some people naturally have more efficient systems than others. The good news for us is that these limits can be pushed back by training. We will look at some very important concepts to do with these limits

and performance in sport and physical activity next.

Tasks

1 In the picture below, the arms and the legs have both got big, thick arteries and veins. Explain why you think our limbs need such a good blood supply.
2 Explain why you think you measure your pulse as a test for fitness.
3 Smoking causes lung disease and heart disease. Design a poster to persuade people to stop smoking.

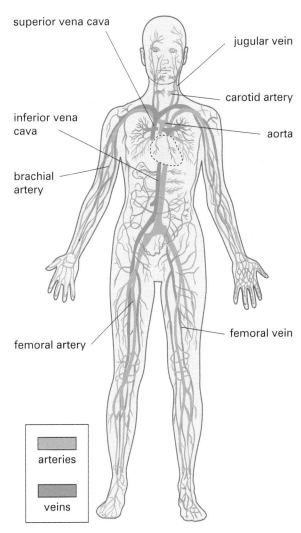

How blood gets around the body: the main veins and arteries of the circulatory system

Circulation and respiration: participation and performance

Lactic acid

We know that muscles need oxygen to work effectively. Remember, though, that in anaerobic exercise muscles can work for a short time without oxygen (see page 13 to remind yourself). When the supply of oxygen to muscles becomes insufficient for the work they are being asked to do, muscles have to find a new source of energy. This is done by converting the energy we store in our bodies (carbohydrates) into **glycogen**. Glycogen is a form of energy that muscles can use without needing oxygen.

However, anaerobic exercise, using glycogen rather than oxygen, can only go on for a short amount of time. This is because when muscles have to work anaerobically, they produce a waste product: a chemical called **lactic acid**. Lactic acid is a poison that stops the muscles working effectively. As muscles continue to work without oxygen, lactic acid gradually builds up. This produces sensations that you will recognise. Muscles begin to ache, and eventually fatigue sets in. The cramp won't go away until the muscle is rested while the blood brings fresh oxygen to it again.

As we have already seen, the body has systems to remove waste products, and lactic acid is slowly processed by the body and turned into carbon dioxide and water. Some of it is eventually turned back into energy. However, the short-term effect is for the build-up of lactic acid to prevent the muscles from working efficiently. This effect increases the harder the muscles are made to work.

The build-up of lactic acid in muscles happens far more quickly in activities requiring short, all-out effort than it does in

When fatigue sets in, it is very difficult to perform effectively

longer, endurance-based activities. This is because in the more endurance-based activities muscles are not working so hard and the body is often able to disperse the lactic acid faster than it accumulates for a more lengthy period.

Oxygen debt

The amount of oxygen reaching our muscles is obviously a big factor affecting performance and participation.

When the rate at which muscles work is greater than the body's ability to supply oxygen, the result is a shortage of oxygen and, inevitably, fatigue. This oxygen shortage is called **oxygen debt**, and it has to be repaid for the muscles to work efficiently again. This is done by taking in great gulps of air until sufficient oxygen has been taken in to allow the removal of lactic acid and the replenishment of muscle energy stores.

Remember: the supply of oxygen to our muscles is limited by our capacity to take in oxygen during a performance and for that oxygen to reach working muscles efficiently.

Duration

The duration and/or the nature of an activity greatly influence both lactic acid accumulation and oxygen debt. Sprinters consume energy very quickly without taking in oxygen (anaerobic exercise), which means that the onset of fatigue occurs very quickly within a matter of seconds. In events of longer duration, fatigue develops much more gradually as the body is able to reprocess some of its lost energy and minimise lactic acid build-up during exercise or competition.

Recovery rate

A sprinter can recover from an all-out effort in around three minutes. This is the time it takes for the accumulation of lactic acid in the muscles to fall to an acceptable level for muscles to start working efficiently again. For most sprinters, part of their training programme will include repetition sprints in order to develop the body's capacity to recover from work quickly.

Sprinters often need to recover from work quickly

Activity of longer duration, such as a marathon or a long-distance cycle ride will, as you might expect, require a considerably longer period of recovery. In this case, the oxygen taken in during recovery is used to remove lactic acid from the muscles that has built up over an extended period. In some instances, it can be several hours before the heart rate and respiratory rate return to normal levels.

Tolerance

The amount of work the body can cope with varies from one individual to another. But it is possible to increase the body's tolerance to lactic acid build-up and oxygen debt by improving fitness. Regular activity that gradually increases in duration and/or intensity will develop and affect the efficiency of the circulatory and respiratory systems.

Improving the amount of oxygen that the lungs can deliver to the blood, making the heart stronger and the blood vessels able to deliver more oxygen to the muscles more efficiently will all increase tolerance. This will delay the onset of muscle fatigue due to lactic acid accumulation, and improve performance and participation. We will look at the benefits of improving the circulatory and respiratory systems next.

Tasks

1. Describe how the build-up of lactic acid occurs in the body's muscles.
2. Explain why it would be important for an athlete to improve their recovery time.
3. Explain why you think you are more likely to get cramp in a games activity on a muddy pitch than on astroturf.

Benefits of exercise: the circulatory system

Exercise is good for us, whether we are training to be top sportspeople or are more interested in PlayStation than playing fields. In today's world, especially in countries like the UK, most people lead a sedentary lifestyle, which means we sit down a lot! It is therefore essential that people take enough regular exercise to stay healthy. For athletes and the general population alike, the benefits of regular activity differ only in the level, intensity and frequency with which they need to be practised.

Stronger cardiac muscle

Cardiac (heart) muscle becomes stronger as a result of regular activity and exercise. As it grows stronger, the heart also increases in size and it is not uncommon for trained athletes to have hearts significantly larger than those of the average population. A stronger and larger heart produces the following desirable effects:

- increased stroke volume
- increased cardiac output
- lower resting heart rate.

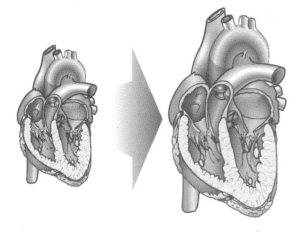

An active heart is bigger, stronger and healthier

Increased stroke volume

Stroke volume is the amount of blood pumped from the heart during a single beat. It is normally measured when an athlete is at rest. Stroke volume may be considerably improved by an extended period of training, particularly in the case of endurance athletes. The greater the stroke volume, the greater the amount of blood pumped around the body for each heartbeat. This should mean more oxygen can be delivered to the muscles and body organs, improving performance (see pages 20–1).

Increased cardiac output

Cardiac means 'of the heart', like cardiac muscle, so **cardiac output** means how much blood the heart pumps out. Cardiac output is measured in terms of the total volume of blood pumped from the heart during one minute.

> *cardiac output =*
> *stroke volume × beats per minute*

In endurance events this increased capacity means that both respiratory and circulation systems work far more efficiently. This allows performance to continue for longer, or at a higher level, or sometimes both.

Lower resting heart rate

A stronger, larger heart pumps more blood around the body each time it beats. This means that it has to work far less hard to achieve the same results as before. In other words, it works far more efficiently. A lower resting heart rate shows that a person has a fit and efficient heart.

Resting heart rates vary between individuals, but they are normally between 60 beats per minute (bpm) and 80 bpm. People who exercise regularly tend to have resting heart rates of between 50–60 bpm. Each time their heart beats, more blood is pumped around the body and so the heart needs to beat less often to achieve the same result as a 'normal' person. Very fit individuals can achieve extremely low resting heart rates. Olympic rowing champion, Steve Redgrave, has a resting heart rate of between 40–45 bpm, while the recently retired Spanish cyclist, Miguel Indurain, has a resting heart rate of just 27 bpm!

Measuring your pulse

To measure your heart rate you need to measure your **pulse**. Every time your heart beats, it pumps out a surge of blood. Where large blood vessels are close to the surface of the skin, you can feel this surge of blood going through the blood vessel. To count the number of times your heart beats a minute (your heart rate), you need to count your pulse over a minute. Or you can be clever and count it for fifteen seconds and multiply the result by four!

The most common places to measure your pulse at are the radial pulse on the inside of your wrist, and the carotid pulse. This is on your neck, just to one side of the Adam's apple (larynx).

Tasks

1. Work out your resting heart rate and keep a record of it.
2. Compare your resting heart rate with the rest of your group. Do people who are good at endurance activities have lower resting heart rates?
3. Using books, magazines and the Internet, if available, research the career of Sir Steven Redgrave. What other factors have affected his performance as an Olympic champion?

What factors might affect the performance of this Olympic champion?

Improving performance: the respiratory system

Gaseous exchange

Air breathed into the lungs contains oxygen. In the lungs, the oxygen passes into the bloodstream. At the same time, carbon dioxide from the blood is transferred into the lungs, and then exhaled (breathed out). Both oxygen and carbon dioxide are gases, and the process of oxygen going into the blood and carbon dioxide leaving the blood is called **gaseous exchange**.

The lungs have a very big surface area. In fact, if you were to flatten your lungs out completely, they would cover over 55 square metres! This massive surface area is needed to make sure as much as possible of the surface of the lungs is in contact with the capillaries of the blood system that surrounds them. This maximises the delivery of oxygen from the lungs to the blood, and the delivery of carbon dioxide from the blood to the lungs.

The lung is largely made up of alveoli. These are tiny sacs surrounded by capillaries. The walls of the alveoli are very thin: just one cell thick, and the walls of the surrounding capillaries are very thin as well: also one cell thick. This makes it easy for gaseous exchange to occur. As we breathe in, the tiny sacs of the alveoli fill with air, as we breathe out, they empty.

The process of gaseous exchange involves both the respiratory and circulatory systems and works more efficiently where blood supply and oxygen are delivered effectively to the lungs. Just as regular exercise brings improvement in the efficiency of the circulatory system, it also has a beneficial effect on the respiratory system. As with the circulatory system, improvements to the respiratory system will have a big effect on performance and participation. More oxygen released into the bloodstream means more oxygen for muscles to use.

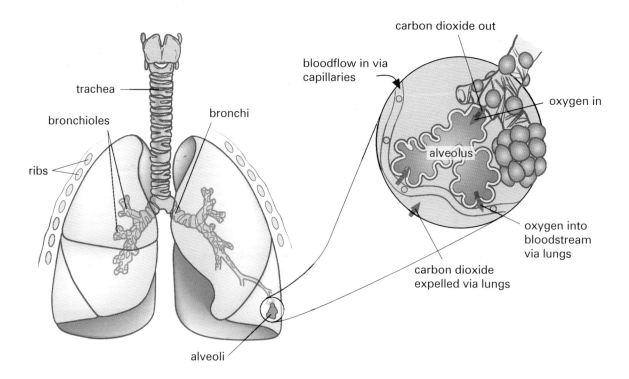

Each lung has approximately 300 million alveoli – 600 million in all!

Benefits from exercise

Regular exercise and training can improve the way the heart functions (see page 24). The same is true for the lungs, and the following improvements can be made in the way they work:

- **increased vital capacity**
- **increased tidal volume**
- **increased oxygen debt tolerance**.

Increased vital capacity

The **vital capacity** of the lungs is quite simply the total volume of air you can move in and out of the lungs in one deep breath – or one complete breathing cycle (breathing in and out). This is measured from the point at which the lungs have expelled as much air as possible (maximum exhalation) through breathing in as much air as possible (maximum inhalation) and back to maximum exhalation again.

For an athlete, increased vital capacity is important because the volume of oxygen that can be inhaled and the amount of carbon dioxide expelled are both factors that influence performance. An increased oxygen supply allows muscles to work harder and/or longer, whilst the increased amount of carbon dioxide expelled delays the build up of lactic acid in the muscles.

Tidal volume

Tidal volume is the amount of air entering and leaving your system with each breath. This is our normal breathing cycle. If you increase the capacity of your lungs through regular exercise, you will also increase your tidal volume – and be able to deliver more oxygen to and remove carbon dioxide from your blood more quickly. The quicker you can remove carbon dioxide, the quicker the blood can take up fresh oxygen again.

Oxygen debt tolerance

Increasing both the oxygen-carrying capacity of the blood and the vital capacity of the lungs means that the body is more able to tolerate oxygen debt during exercise. In endurance activities (aerobic exercise), an athlete will be able to perform for longer, whilst those athletes performing at the anaerobic/aerobic threshold (e.g. 400 metres) will find that increased oxygen debt tolerance will allow them to maintain their performance for slightly longer.

Even short duration event athletes can benefit from such improvements, particularly when they are taking part in several heats or rounds of competition and need to recover effectively within a short space of time.

Task

Measure your vital capacity.
Your teacher will provide the equipment needed for this test, called the bell jar experiment. In this test, you breathe in as much as you can (maximum inhalation), then breathe out as much as you can (maximum exhalation) into a rubber tube. The rubber tube leads into a bell jar filled with water; the air you breathe out will expel water from the bell jar.
Record your result.

Circulatory system	(Bloodflow to and from the heart)
↓	
Activity & exercise	(Improves bloodflow and cardiac capacity)
↓	
Gaseous exchange	O_2 into lungs– CO_2 out via lungs
↑	
Activity & exercise	(Improves lung capacity and efficiency)
↑	
Respiratory system	(Oxygen intake and removal of CO_2 and waste products)

The blood and physical activity

Blood has three primary functions, all of which become accelerated during physical activity:

- **transport**
- **protection**
- **regulation.**

All three of these functions of the blood are very important factors affecting performance and participation.

Transport

Blood transports oxygen from the lungs to the body's tissues and carbon dioxide back to the lungs to be exhaled. It carries dissolved food from the gut to various parts of the body and waste products to the kidneys from where they are excreted in urine. Blood also carries hormones and antibodies around the body. The efficient transportation of oxygen is very important to the athlete (see page 20).

Protection

Blood contains clotting agents that help to stop bleeding when we sustain cuts or grazes. Blood also contains **white blood cells** that protect us against infection.

Platelets are also carried in the blood. These platelets promote blood clotting. Blood clotting helps prevent severe blood loss following an injury or cut. This can be a risk for those who take part in contact sports.

There is a medical condition called haemophilia, which is a disease that reduces the ability of the blood to clot. People with haemophilia have to be very careful not to cut themselves, which reduces their ability to participate in activities such as contact sports were they might be at risk.

Regulation

Blood also helps to regulate the body's temperature. The veins and capillaries close to the skin expand in order to lose heat and contract when it is necessary to retain heat to keep warm. Skin temperature affects blood temperature in the vessels close to the surface of the skin and this temperature change is then circulated throughout the body.

The body also has other mechanisms that help regulate temperature, because the body systems will not function properly if a person gets too hot or too cold.

Components of blood

Blood is made up of several different components: **red blood cells**, white blood cells, platelets and **plasma**.

Red blood cells

Red blood cells carry oxygen to where the body needs it. They are essential in the transporting role of blood. These blood cells are red because they contain a substance called **haemoglobin**.

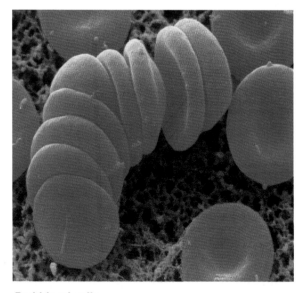

Red blood cells

Haemoglobin attracts oxygen, so when blood passes through the capillaries surrounding the alveoli, oxygen moves from the lungs to the red blood cells.

It seems logical that the more red blood cells you have, the more oxygen you are able to deliver to your muscles. People who live in mountainous areas tend to have more red blood cells because the air is thinner at altitude and so their blood has to be more efficient at taking oxygen from the lungs. This is why athletes often train in high altitude areas, and why athletes from high altitude areas are often exceptional at long distance and endurance events.

Some people suffer from a condition called **anaemia**, which means they have fewer red blood cells than normal. This condition, like haemophilia, can sometimes limit participation in sport and physical activity, because not enough oxygen can be carried to the muscles.

This athlete is from Kenya, a country with excellent conditions for high altitude training

White blood cells

White blood cells are the body's main defence against infection and disease. They are an important part of the blood's protective function. White blood cells are transparent cells that swim around in the blood plasma. They can swallow up bacteria and viruses and digest them. Some can also produce antibodies that protect the body from infection.

Platelets

Platelets help with blood clotting. They are tiny cell fragments and when a blood vessel is cut the platelets swell up and become sticky, clogging up the cut and preventing blood loss. If the cut is too big to block in this way, the body has another system to help prevent blood loss. The brain sends a chemical signal to contract the blood vessels around the cut, so that the flow of blood in that area is reduced.

Plasma

Plasma is a liquid, mainly made up of water. It allows the blood to flow. It also carries digested foods in soluble form and hormones such as insulin and adrenaline. Waste products such as carbon dioxide and uric acid are carried in plasma, so it is an essential part of gaseous exchange.

Tasks

1. Where is blood made? (see page 6 for the answer!)
2. Do you think it's fair for an athlete with a naturally high red blood cell count to compete against athletes with naturally lower red blood cell counts? Discuss this in groups.
3. Investigate the illegal practice of blood doping. Use books, CD-ROMs and the Internet, if you have access to it. Write a short report explaining what it does.

Aerobic and anaerobic activity

The circulatory system and the respiratory system work together as a crucial factor affecting performance and participation. We have seen how muscles must have oxygen in order to work effectively. The circulatory and respiratory systems work together to supply the body with oxygen and to take away the waste products released when the body cells produce energy. Activity fuelled by oxygen is called aerobic activity.

We have also seen, though, that it is possible for muscles to work without oxygen for short periods of time. When the demands made on muscles are greater than the ability of the circulatory and respiratory systems to supply them with oxygen, muscles can use glycogen to work. However, this comes at a price: lactic acid and oxygen debt. Activity fuelled without oxygen is called anaerobic activity.

In these two pages we will round off the topic of the respiratory and circulatory systems by looking at examples of aerobic and anaerobic activities. In your exam you will probably be asked to write about how aerobic and anaerobic conditions affect performance in different types of sport and physical activities, and to give examples. You should think about your own activities, and how the different ways that muscles can work affects your own performance.

Endurance events (mostly aerobic)

What allows endurance athletes to make their muscles work over long periods of time is aerobic fitness. In endurance events, the body must work at a level that allows the removal of waste products (including lactic acid) at a rate greater than that at which they accumulate. This, of course, cannot go on indefinitely, and is limited by the body's stored energy reserves and its ability to delay the onset of oxygen debt and lactic acid accumulation. We have seen that the way to delay oxygen debt and lactic acid build-up is to improve the fitness of the heart so it can pump blood more efficiently; improve the capacity of the lungs, so more oxygen can be delivered with less effort; and improve the ability of the blood to carry oxygen.

In a 1500-metre swimming race, for example, the swimmer must swim at a speed that can be maintained for the duration of the race. This will be determined by the rate at which the body can operate without becoming exhausted. If the swimmer attempts to keep up with a faster opponent, he or she may do so at the expense of a declining level of performance later in the race.

In endurance swimming muscles have to work for a long time

Speed and power events (mostly anaerobic)

Anaerobic activity is entirely different from aerobic activity, as it involves the performance of work without oxygen. Activities such as sprinting, throwing and jumping events in athletics and weightlifting require maximum effort, which pushes muscles into short term anaerobic work.

Maximum muscular effort in action!

In many such activities, repeated performances are required. The weightlifter may take the stage having decided upon their opening weight and is allowed three attempts in total during the competition. This is where recovery is very important (see page 23). The athlete must make a full recovery between each attempt so that the body is ready for the next exertion.

Sometimes (as in major competitions) there may be a considerable delay between rounds and this allows a full warm-up both before and after each performance. However, the delay may be as short as ten or fifteen minutes. In such instances it is common for massage and other physical techniques to be used in order to speed up the removal of lactic acid prior to the next performance.

Aerobic and anaerobic!

In the UK, as in many parts of the world, team games are very popular. Rugby, soccer, hockey, basketball and netball at times all require short bursts of maximum energy, such as in sprinting to reach a pass or beat an opponent to the ball. At other times players may be moving at a much slower pace when they are not in possession of the ball or are not directly involved in play at that moment.

The limit of anaerobic work is normally around 40 seconds and after that the aerobic energy system takes over again. This is known as the **anaerobic threshold**. In team games the body must 'switch' from one type of work to another and back again several times.

Training

Endurance activities and speed and power activities require training designed to improve either aerobic fitness and anaerobic fitness. This will increase the amount of oxygen reaching muscles for aerobic activities, and increase the body's tolerance to oxygen debt for anaerobic activities. Sports that require switching between aerobic and anaerobic work will need to train to improve fitness for both. We will look at training methods in detail on page 114.

Tasks

1. Think of *two* events or games where performers use mainly aerobic energy.
2. Think of *two* events or games where performers use mainly anaerobic energy.
3. Many people go to aerobics classes. Explain why are these called 'aerobics'.

Tennis: an anaerobic *and* aerobic activity

Skill

Skill has been defined as:

The learned ability to bring about predetermined results with maximum certainty, often with the minimum outlay of time or energy or both. (Guthrie, 1956)

Although this definition is now more than forty years old, it still conveys the essential points that skill is something that:

- you learn
- you can (eventually) do predictably and consistently
- you can perform efficiently.

Feedback

Feedback is the information received by a competitor either *during* or *after* a performance. When this information is positive and helpful it can enable a performer to alter and improve performance. In some cases this may be possible during a game or in the next attempt at a gymnastics event, for example. Sometimes feedback is useful in analysing faults for subsequent work in training, which may bring improved results in later competition.

Feedback can take several forms. For your GCSE course, you need to know about:

- **intrinsic feedback**
- **extrinsic feedback**
- **knowledge of performance (KP)**
- **knowledge of results (KR).**

Intrinsic feedback

Experienced performers are able to recognise some faults in their own performance. This is

intrinsic feedback – having enough experience to see how you can improve your own performance. How good intrinsic feedback is depends on the experience and self-knowledge of the performer. Beginners who are making mistakes may not have sufficient knowledge to enable them to correct them without assistance, while advanced performers are more likely to be able to do so.

Many sporting skills are learned progressively and should be acquired under guidance

Extrinsic feedback

Feedback that comes from someone else, rather than the performer concerned, is called **extrinsic feedback**. Teachers, coaches, even spectators can supply advice on how to improve to a performer or to a team who, depending upon their experience, may act upon it – or not!

Extrinsic feedback can take the form of general encouragement from spectators, or more specific information, such as the tactical analysis that might be part of the half-time team talk in rugby, football or hockey. Extrinsic feedback also includes feedback from a coach, trainer or even a PE teacher during practice or training. It would also be the kind of feedback you would give on someone else's performance during the analysis of performance part of your course.

To be effective, it is particularly important that external feedback:

- is restricted to one or two specific comments at a time
- does not confuse or de-motivate the athlete
- occurs either during competition or as soon as possible afterwards.

Knowledge of performance (KP)

Although **knowledge of performance** can come from an athlete's own perception of their performance, it is more likely to be obtained from external sources such as the coach or through the use of video replays. Knowledge of performance means analysing the nature of the performance and working out how it may be improved – irrespective of results. Even if a performer is successful there are likely to be minor points of technique (or tactics) that can be refined in order to further improve performance.

Video of a performance can be a useful and impartial analytical tool

Knowledge of results comes from external sources

Knowledge of results (KR)

Knowledge of results is not quite the same as knowledge of performance. This form of feedback comes from external sources, such as the result of a game, the judges' score in a judo competition or the distance recorded in a javelin throw. Athletes and sportspeople can learn from the result or outcome of a competition. This is just one measure of how well – or poorly – they are performing, either as individuals or as part of a team.

For example, a soccer or hockey team may be conceding lots of goals or a golfer may be consistently recording scores above 'par'.

This form of feedback is helpful where results indicate poor performance more readily than the nature of the performance itself.

Tasks

1. For one of your chosen activities, practise *intrinsic* feedback and identify one skill you need to improve in.
2. With a partner, practise *extrinsic* feedback for an activity you have both chosen. Identify one skill that you think needs to be improved, and feed back to your partner.

Open and closed skills

In your coursework you will be working on developing and applying advanced skills in your four chosen activities. You may also have the opportunity to write about these advanced skills in the exam. In the exam, you will be asked about **open skills** and **closed skills**. The difference between them is very important, and thinking of the skills you are developing as either open or closed may help you improve in your coursework.

Closed skills

Some skills are fairly fixed: they require little or no adjustment during competition. Once learned, they remain essentially the same, although of course they can be adapted and refined in order to make them more effective. These are known as closed skills. Closed skills may require countless hours of work in order to perfect them to a high degree. A particular golf shot, hurdling in athletics, running, cycling, putting the shot or pole vaulting all come into the category of closed skills. Some of these examples involve fairly simple skills whilst others require much more complex ones.

What makes a closed skill fairly fixed is that the performer is in control of most factors of the environment in which they are performing. Trampolining is a good example; there will not be any great variation in the environment (the equipment and its surroundings) in which the performer has trained to perfect their skills and the one in which they are now performing competitively.

Putting the shot is also a closed skill, but here the performer is slightly less in control of the environment. The performer will have spent hundreds of hours practising and improving the closed skill of putting the shot and will be using the same standard equipment. However, wind strength and direction is not under the performer's control and they may need to alter their skill slightly to achieve a good performance.

Pole vaulting is another closed skill, but in the run-up, wind speed and direction will have even more of an influence on performance, and the performer will have to adjust their skill accordingly.

In each of these cases, however, these closed skills can be practised over and over again and modified until they become consistent and effective. Where adjustments need to be made, they involve only slight alterations in technique or application of the skill.

There is often an assumption that closed skills are also simple skills. This is very rarely so: even running, which seems so simple, takes us years to learn as we are growing up. Most closed skills require hundreds of hours of attention to the tiniest detail in order to perfect them.

Pole vaulting is a closed skill but it is certainly not simple

Open skills

In contrast, some sporting skills need to be constantly adapted or modified during play. This is because the environment of play or performance is not under the performer's control: usually because there are other people involved. These are known as open skills.

Take basketball, for example. A pass in basketball may be made over a distance of just a few feet or almost the whole length of the court. The reason why this is an open skill is that the performer is passing to someone else, and trying to keep the ball away from all the people on the other team. A pass in basketball is therefore an open skill: the performer cannot control what will happen next.

In hockey, the way in which a hockey ball is controlled and passed will depend on its speed of arrival, the proximity of team mates and the likelihood of a challenge being made by an opposing player. So ball control in hockey is also an open skill and it has to be constantly adapted to the changing circumstances of the game.

Adapting skills

Many sports skills cannot be learned as closed or fixed skills. They need to be adapted to changing situations with the player able to react quickly in adjusting the skill to meet the precise circumstances.

Some activities require performers to perfect both open and closed skills. A place kick in rugby is a closed skill which many players practise for hours in order to perfect their technique. Other skills in the game require constant adaptation during play.

You will need to identify both closed and open skills, particularly in the activities you have chosen to present at practical moderation.

Tasks

1. For *two* of your activities, identify a closed skill. Using intrinsic feedback, think about how both skills could be improved.
2. With a partner, identify *two* open skills in *two* activities you are both doing. Using extrinsic feedback, suggest how each of these four skills could be improved.

Some skills have to be altered according to a particular situation

Skill and ability

Michael Owen – was he born a great footballer, or are his football skills the result of excellent coaching? There is much debate about whether a good sportsperson is born or is developed as a result of excellent teaching or coaching. The truth probably lies somewhere between the two. But basic abilities are undoubtedly very important as a foundation for developing advanced skills.

Ability is an indicator of potential

Ability

Ability is innate – which means that we are born with it. Some people are naturally faster, more co-ordinated, more artistic or mathematical than others. You'll probably have noticed that, luckily for us all, few people are naturally good at everything!

The type of natural ability that is useful in any physical activity will depend very much on the nature of the activity. Sometimes physical characteristics may be very important. A highly co-ordinated prop forward is of little use to a rugby team if he or she weighs less than the team's scrum-half.

Where natural ability is present and is identified at an early time, it does provide a good basis for the development of those abilities into advanced skills in sport and physical activity. These natural abilities include:

- **speed**
- **agility**
- **co-ordination**
- **flexibility**
- **balance**
- **reaction time.**

A young person who shows a natural flexibility, for example, may be more likely to develop advanced skills as a gymnast more quickly than one who has a limited range of movement. A would-be sprinter who possesses natural speed and quickness of reaction may be more likely to develop advanced skills through coaching and technical refinement than one who doesn't possess either.

While natural ability may make developing advanced skills easier, it can also get in the way. People who are naturally good at something might feel they don't need to work to improve. Such people don't tend to be very successful in their chosen sport or activity. Few people are born with advanced skills – they nearly always have to be learned!

There are other factors that are also important in whether someone goes on to develop advanced skills, and continue to improve performance. Physical type or size is sometimes important, but perhaps the most crucial factor is a positive attitude to training and a desire to improve. Many people who have become top performers were not the most naturally gifted of their generation, but still managed to achieve success through sheer hard work and dedication.

Speed and reaction time

As a natural ability, speed is important in many sports and physical activities. There are two main kinds of speed in sport: how quickly a performer can move and how quick their reactions are. They often come together – in the 100m, for example, performers have to react extremely quickly to the starting gun, and then move extremely quickly!

We will look in a later unit (see page 101) at how you can test for speed, and what you can do to improve your speed. As a natural ability, speed tends to come from having a higher proportion of fast-twitch muscle fibres (see page 13) in the muscles, which allows them to react more quickly and powerfully (and anaerobically). It also comes from general body shape and size (see page 86).

Agility

Agility is the ability to move quickly and flexibly. In judo, for example, performers need to move quickly and accurately, changing direction and reacting quickly to their competitor's movements. Have you ever heard the expression that a goalkeeper in football is 'like a cat'? Goalkeepers have to be extremely agile, throwing themselves in all directions to make a save as in the picture below.

Goalkeepers have to be extremely agile

Agility is also inherited in terms of the flexibility of your joints and your body shape and size. We will be looking at tests for agility and ways it can be improved.

Co-ordination

Co-ordination is control over movement and being able to link different movements together effectively and easily. It is a vital ability for good performance as sport and physical activity is all about controlling movement in particular ways.

Flexibility

Flexibility is the amount you can bend or stretch your joints (see pages 101–102). It is an essential part of activities like dance and gymnastics, but is very important in all sport and physical activity because greater flexibility allows more efficient and effective joint movement, and reduces the chance of injury. We will be looking at tests for and ways of improving flexibility. You inherit your flexibility, and you tend to become less flexible as you get older. This is one reason why champion gymnasts are often very young.

Balance

Balance, like co-ordination, is also to do with controlling body movement: retaining balance when moving or standing still. Tests for balance are covered on page 103.

Tasks

1. For each of the abilities listed here, identify *two* sporting activities for which that ability is an important factor affecting performance.
2. Choose *one* of your activities. If you were a talent spotter for that activity, what abilities would you look for?
3. When does an ability become a skill? Discuss this question in groups.

Different levels of skill

Someone quite new to a sport (a novice) and a top level performer in that sport will have learned the same basic skills, but they will not perform them to the same standard. We know that skill can be defined as something that:

- you learn
- you can (eventually) do predictably and consistently
- you can perform efficiently.

Advanced skills and techniques are not learned overnight and must be developed stage by stage. What makes the skills of the novice different from those of the top level performer is the way in which they are performed.

The novice may well:

- be very inconsistent in how well they perform a new skill each time they try it
- put a lot of effort in but produce a less effective performance
- not perform the skill as quickly or efficiently
- not be able to adapt the skill quickly when necessary, or may not possess the experience needed to do this.

The top level performer, however:

- will demonstrate a high level of consistency with each performance
- will perform the skill with apparently little effort or energy expenditure
- will perform the skill quickly and efficiently (manage time)
- will be capable of adapting the skill to meet precise situations as they arise (be **adaptable**).

The key words to remember, then, are:

- **consistency**
- **energy**
- **time**
- **adaptable**.

Learning and developing skill

In order to learn or improve skills we normally undergo practice, coaching or teaching sessions. If we are to make progress, these should be specially designed to improve our level of skill or a particular aspect of it.

As in other areas of learning, you can learn some simple skills in one go (like catching a

What makes the skills of a novice different from the skills of a top performer?

ball), and continue to improve that skill by practising it. This is called **whole learning**. Other skills may be more complicated and may need to be broken down and learned as a series of 'mini-skills' before they are attempted in their entirety. This is called **part learning**.

Whether we learn skills by attempting them as a whole or as a series of smaller skills that can eventually be joined together, we use the same sort of ways of learning, refining and adapting the skill. These usually involve:

- **demonstration**
- **copying**
- **practice**
- **trial and error**
- **role models.**

Demonstration and copying

Skills are learned by copying other people: sports stars on TV, your teacher or trainer, your friends. A teacher or coach will demonstrate how a skill should be performed, and then feed back on a student's performance until it's being done correctly. Advanced skills can be taught in the same way: here, though, the demonstrator needs to know the sport very well for it to be effective. Video or film footage can also be used.

Practice

Skills become established or 'grooved' as a result of practice. For practice to be effective, it must be based upon correct procedures. Therefore any demonstration must be technically correct. Feedback is also essential, both from the performer (*intrinsic*) and from coaches and/or teachers (*extrinsic*). There is an old saying that 'practice makes perfect', but it would be better to remember that 'perfect practice makes *perfect*'!

Practice can be based on the whole skill, or in some cases on one aspect of it, but in either case, this needs to be based upon correct technique. Aimless practice or practice which does not reinforce good habits is not very effective. A good demonstration model is needed so that performers have a constant reference against which to compare their own efforts.

Trial and error

Trial and error means doing something until you happen to hit on a way that makes it work. The trial and error method of learning and practice can produce problems, particularly if it is undertaken over a long period of time and with little knowledge of what is actually correct in terms of technique. Bad habits are difficult to break later on.

Just 'having a go' is of course better than not taking part at all in physical activity, but for those who do wish to learn skills correctly for whatever reason, this form of practice is not likely to produce the best results.

Role models

Role models (stars in a particular sport or activity) can be very useful in demonstrating skills. To be useful in learning skills, the role model has to be a good technical role model, but to be a good role model a person should also promote the sport in their conduct both on and off the field of play.

Tasks

1. For one of your activities, identify one skill that could be learned as a whole skill, and one that would be best learned in parts first.
2. Why is it essential for learning skills that skill demonstrations are of a high standard? Discuss in groups.
3. Imagine you are a coach. Write a letter to yourself saying how you could improve your performance.

Learning skills: information processing

While we are learning skills and when we execute them during competition, we are **processing information**. Some of this information has been stored in our memory and consists of what we have learned so far and what we remember of past experiences. During a competition or match we need to process the following information about the present situation:

- what is happening (input)
- how do we react to it (decision-making /output)
- was the right reaction used? (feedback)

For example, in tennis each player has to watch what their opponent is doing, react to it by selecting a shot or moving to a new position on the court, and then see if that reaction was the right one. If they want to win or improve their performance, the player must remember whether they made the correct reaction or not, so they can do it again or try something else the next time a similar situation occurs.

Both during competition and afterwards we will receive further information from coaches, trainers, etc about how we performed. This is added to our own perception of how we performed (feedback – see pages 32–3) and it will be added to our store of memory for future occasions. It is this whole system that allows us to adapt and refine skills as we use them. It also allows us to get the information we need to identify strengths and weaknesses and improve our performance.

The model on the opposite page shows this process in action in a competitive situation. It is for tennis again, but it works for almost any game or competitive situation.

Wrong decision!

Input

At all times a performer must pay attention to what is going on around him or her and how this might affect their role in the game or competition. This might mean watching the speed or flight of the ball or whether it is likely to bounce awkwardly.

Decision-making

A performer must make decisions about which pass to make, whether to tackle, where to move and when, dependent upon how he or she sees the situation (input).

Output

Output is the result of both input and decision-making: selecting the appropriate skill; the right pass; being in the right place at the right time, etc.

Feedback

Having executed the selected skill, the player will see whether or not the response was a) the correct one and b) whether it was successful. This information will be added to that already stored in the memory and should influence any future decision-making if similar input situations happen again.

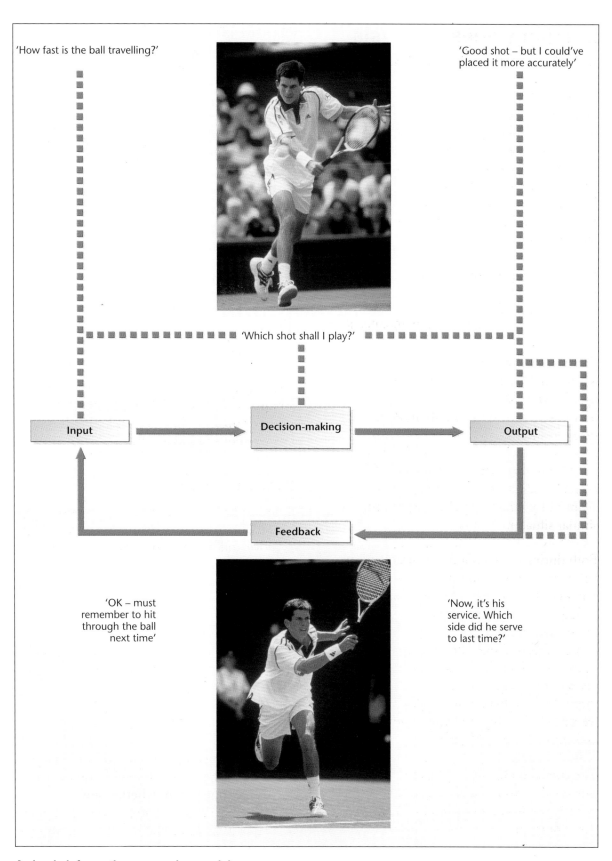

'How fast is the ball travelling?'

'Good shot – but I could've placed it more accurately'

'Which shot shall I play?'

| Input | Decision-making | Output |

Feedback

'OK – must remember to hit through the ball next time'

'Now, it's his service. Which side did he serve to last time?'

A simple information processing model

Evaluation and analysis

You can only improve skills and performance if you know what's wrong with them, and how this might be put right. The key words here are **evaluation**, **analysis** and planning for improvement. Evaluation means being able to see what is good and bad about a performance. Analysis means breaking down a performance in order to evaluate it effectively. Planning for improvement means knowing what can be done to improve a performance and putting these things into practice.

To maximise the chances of improvement, evaluation, analysis and planning need to been done regularly and thoroughly. Ideally, they should be done by someone who is an expert in the sport or activity and who can be objective about the performance – someone who knows what they are doing.

This means, of course, feedback, which is central to evaluation, analysis and planning for improvement. We have seen already (on pages 32–3) that there are four main kinds of feedback: intrinsic and extrinsic, knowledge of performance (KP) and knowledge of results (KR). We can now add to this that for feedback to be really effective, it needs to come from someone who has specialised knowledge of:

- skill-learning processes
- group and/or individual skills relevant to the sport
- aspects of fitness relevant to the sport
- tactics and strategies relevant to the sport.

Communicating feedback effectively is a very important skill

Someone giving feedback really needs to know how skills are learned and improved. This means that they can plan effectively for improvement. They need to know all about the skills required for the game or activity and how they should be performed.

The person giving feedback also needs to know about the fitness requirements for the sport or activity, in order to identify whether fitness needs to be improved and suggest ways of doing this. In addition, they need to know all about the tactics and strategies of the game or activity. This is important as it enables them to analyse and evaluate all aspects of performance and help to plan for improvement.

Feedback provides the information required to identify group or individual faults and errors in performance. However, it must be used in a meaningful and constructive way for it to have a positive effect.

Some coaches are excellent at evaluating and analysing performance, but not so good at communicating the information back to the performers. Communicating feedback effectively is a very important process.

In sport today, videos are often made of a performance and are then used to support feedback. The advantage of videotaping a performance and reviewing the tape is that both the coach and the performer receive an unbiased view of skill and performance levels. This is important in ensuring that both the performer and the coach can see an accurate record of any errors or faults.

Analysing performance task

Part of your coursework includes an analysing performance task. For this, you will be asked to apply your skills of analysis in a practical

situation – either analysing someone else's performance or your own. This is your chance to apply your specialist knowledge of the activity, and also to apply the knowledge you now have on factors affecting performance and how skills are learned.

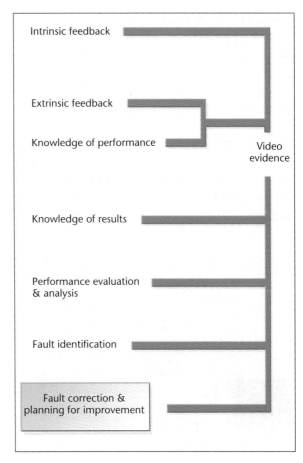

Feedback is a critical component of fault correction and improvement

Tasks

1. Apply the information processing model on page 41 to a specific moment in one of your activities. List the input, decisions, output and feedback you made.
2. List the factors that help improve skills.
3. If everyone could video their own performance, would we still need coaches? Discuss this in groups.

Motivation and mental preparation

Mental preparation

No matter how skilful or gifted someone may be physically, this can count for nothing if they are not prepared for competition *mentally*. Lack of preparation, concern about current form and loss of confidence can all have a negative effect upon performance and participation.

Performance is often closely associated with pressure: performers are tested by their opponents both physically and mentally, and when people are watching the performance this adds to the pressure to perform well. Some performers actually do better when they are under pressure, and this is often the sign of a champion in sport. For others, a competition or big event causes anxiety and stress, which can make them perform badly.

Mental preparation is a necessary part of modern-day sporting performance. In order to be able to approach a competition or game in the right frame of mind, a performer needs to be confident that they are as well prepared as possible. In sport today, there are very few top performers who do not use outside assistance to help them prepare mentally for competition. This preparation often contains three key elements:

- **relaxation**
- **mental rehearsal**
- **focusing.**

Relaxation

The mind and the body are very closely intertwined, so relaxation should involve both mental relaxation and physical relaxation.

Physical relaxation means reducing the muscular tension that often builds up before a big event or competition. Muscular tension comes from psychological tension – stress and anxiety about performance.

Getting it right in the mind is a necessary component of a good performance

The physical relaxation of muscles is often dealt with by massage and manipulation techniques but care must be taken that performers do not become *too* relaxed immediately prior to a competition. They need to be sharp, alert and focused.

Mental relaxation is achieved in different ways but can include the playing of calming music, meditation, quiet talking with a coach or friend, going for a walk, or 'self-talk' – where the athlete goes through a prepared routine of self-communication using certain key words as part of their preparation.

Spectators can add to the pressure on performers

Mental rehearsal

The ability to picture what a skill should look like when performed well is an important part of learning that skill (see page 40). Performers also use mental imagery (pictures) to prepare for competitions. Key aspects of the performance or specific skill are pictured mentally so that they are fixed firmly in place before the competition begins. These images should be positive, with the athlete seeing him or herself performing well and feeling positive.

Mental rehearsal also means going through what you want to achieve in a performance. A weightlifter, for example, might go through the stages of the lift and hold, picturing each stage as they want to perform it.

This practice builds up the performer's confidence, as they will approach the competitive situation with these key aspects well rehearsed both physically and mentally.

Focusing

Focusing is closely related to mental rehearsal. An individual athlete, for example, may need to run through certain key points of technique to ensure they are clearly understood and remembered. Or a team may have certain tactical approaches, which need to remain uppermost in their minds. The

mind should be free from distractions, with thoughts focused upon the main aims of the competition or game: a personal best, the need to qualify for the next round, to maintain composure, etc.

The purpose of a focusing process is to identify a few key points which, if achieved, should ensure success. This is not the time to catalogue a whole list of aims and objectives – that will simply be confusing and de-motivating.

Focusing also helps performers ignore the sights and sounds around them: the noise of the crowd, the panel of judges in front of them, worries about other aspects of their life, or concerns about their performance. Instead, they are able just to concentrate on what they are about to do, and on doing it as well as they can. Some performers call this state of mind being 'in the zone'.

Tasks

1. Make a list of the factors that could put pressure on performers.
2. Pick a skill for one of your chosen activities. Choose one you don't feel that confident about. Picture yourself performing it perfectly.
3. Which do you think is more important for good performance: physical preparation or mental preparation? List your reasons.

What is motivation?

Motivation is the desire to perform well. Different people are motivated by different things, though there are some common features. The motivation of someone who is training to win an Olympic gold will be different from that of a person who jogs to keep fit and healthy.

While it would probably be impossible to list all the reasons why people are motivated to take part in sport and physical activity, we do know that there are two forms of motivation called:

- **intrinsic** (internal) **motivation**
- **extrinsic** (external) **motivation**.

Intrinsic motivation comes from *inside* the participant; **extrinsic motivation** comes from the *outside*: the result of some external influence. It is of course entirely possible that some people may be motivated by a combination of intrinsic *and* extrinsic reasons.

Intrinsic motivation

Intrinsic motivation is self-motivation. It's the desire of the performer to participate for their own personal reasons: to have fun, to keep fit, to enjoy playing with other people, for the satisfaction of performing well, to prove something to themselves or meet personal goals.

This type of motivation is often associated with those who do not necessarily hope to compete at a top level, but simply enjoy taking part in sport. However, top level performers in many sports are still motivated by a love of what they do, in addition to other, more material rewards.

Extrinsic motivation

Extrinsic motivation is motivation that comes from outside our own personal drives. The

The London Marathon: thousands of people take part just to prove that they can do it!

possibility of winning cups, trophies and medals, the high salaries, prize money and the prospect of personal glory or fame can be significant motivating influences.

Some top level professionals, such as the former WBO world middleweight boxing champion, Chris Eubank, have said money was the main motivation for their continuing to compete. Most sportspeople, though, are driven at least as much by their personal motivations as by the financial reward.

Coaches, teachers and sports governing bodies also use various extrinsic motivators in order to promote and generate interest in a whole range of sporting activities. Award schemes, certificates and badges are now commonplace in schools and sports clubs, as well as other initiatives such as 'High Fives' rugby and 'Quick Cricket', which are designed to get young people interested in those sports.

For most people, participation at any level is usually the result of a mixture of intrinsic and extrinsic influences. You might get great personal satisfaction from learning about what factors affect performance (intrinsic motivation), but you might also be motivated by a desire for a good grade in your PE GCSE (extrinsic), to take just one example!

Chris Eubank: extrinsically motivated?

Arousal

Motivation is also an effective way of stimulating the level of **arousal**, or state of readiness, in a performer. This state of arousal is important prior to and during competition. Coaches or captains 'psyching up' their team before a game are examples of this. Players might be reminded that a championship or a cup final place is at stake in order to raise their level of arousal so that they compete effectively.

For professional sportsmen and women, prize money or the prospects of a gold medal and the media contracts that will follow are enough to ensure that they are ready to give their best at the right time. At a lower level, the thought of the team's picture in the local press or having your name called out (for the right reasons) at a school assembly can produce the necessary arousal prior to a game.

These factors can also act as extrinsic motivators in the longer term.

Over-arousal

Some performers are aroused very easily – in some cases all too easily – and this can cause problems. John McEnroe, a tennis star of the 1970s and 1980s, is still as well known for his tendency to 'lose it' on court as he is remembered for his excellent tennis. Coaches and those in charge of performers at whatever level have to take great care in the way that individuals prepare for competition, whether or not they are part of a team.

Tasks

1. What is the difference between *intrinsic* and *extrinsic* motivation? List three examples of both types.
2. Is there anything wrong with just being in a sport 'for the money'? Discuss this in groups.
3. Design a set of extrinsic motivators to increase participation in a sport of your choice in your community.

John McEnroe: quite often guilty of being 'over-aroused'!

Goal setting

Goal setting is something you may already be familiar with from your Key Stage 3 PE course. It is a process where achievable goals are set by you and your teacher for you to reach as you work on improving your performance.

Setting achievable goals or targets in this way helps increase motivation. It is easier to work towards lots of smaller goals than to work towards one big goal that may be years in the future. Achieving your goals gives a feeling of satisfaction and achievement: a very motivating feeling indeed!

Goal setting can also reduce the level of anxiety about performance, particularly in young or novice performers. Goals may be set which enable a performer to focus on a particular aspect of their activity that needs improving rather than all of it. Goal setting breaks down the area of concern into manageable, less threatening chunks.

SMARTER

For all these reasons, goals should be set bearing in mind the **SMARTER** principles. This word stands for:

S Specific – a specific goal, not a vague desire to improve

M Measurable – there's a standard to measure progress against

A Accepted – the goal is agreed by both performer and coach

R Realistic – it's possible to achieve

T Time-related – a specific time period gives the goal added focus

E Exciting – motivating and interesting

R Recorded – you can see what you've achieved and chart your progress

In activities such as the hammer-throw, which is a very complex skill, there may be several aspects of technique that need attention or improvement. Breaking down the skill into parts and setting specific goals for each part allows each small fault or target to be addressed in a way and at a pace with which the performer is comfortable.

> **Example:**
> A long-jumper with a personal best of 6m 20cm and her coach agree that a long-term aim of 7m is realistic but not achievable for some time.
> A goal for the forthcoming season is set at 6m 40cm, which both believe is achievable and realistic.

It is more likely that improvements will be made if realistic rather than unrealistic targets are set, or a whole series of faults are tackled all at the same time. This causes both confusion and anxiety to the performer.

Your teacher will help you set goals to improve your performance

Both beginners and experienced performers are also much more likely to be motivated if the targets or goals they are set are seen to be achievable within a sensible period of time.

Types of goal

There are two main types of goals in goal setting:

- **process goals**
- **target goals.**

Process goals are usually connected with improvements in technique or skill or some small aspect of them as well as tactics. **Target goals** identify specific targets in overall performance, such as an improving a personal best or increasing the goals scored by a football team. They are also known as outcome goals.

Often, both these types of goal are related. In order to improve on a personal best, it may be necessary to make adjustments to technique or work on strength improvements (process goals) in order that target goals may become achievable.

Goal setting for practical activities

Your GCSE course gives you a very good opportunity to put goal setting into practice. Your teacher will have a copy of the Coursework Guidance Booklet for your course. It lists all the skills you will be marked on for your performance of your practical activities. Also in this book are the activity area criteria for your activity area, whether it's Games, Gymnastics, Dance, Athletics, Outdoor Adventurous, Swimming or Exercise Activities.

The activity area criteria give a mark range for different levels of performance. For example, an excellent performance would get you between 21 and 25 marks.

Your teacher may provide you with a photocopy of the skills list and the criteria for your four activities. You can use these for goal setting.

Read through the skills you will be tested on and highlight those that you think you need to improve. Talk with your teacher about ways you can work on these skills and then set goals for your training.

Remember the SMARTER principle – don't try to take too much on at one time.

Example of goal-setting for basketball:

S **Specific:** improve my ability to dribble with either hand

M **Measurable:** dribble the ball with my left hand for the length of the court

A **Accepted:** I've agreed this goal with my teacher

R **Realistic:** yes – I can already dribble for half the court

T **Time-related:** by half term

E **Exciting:** yes!

R **Recorded:** my teacher and I will keep a record of my progress

Tasks

1. Study the criteria for your activity area. What mark range do you think you are in now? What mark range could you achieve by the end of the course?
2. Set goals with your teacher to improve your weaker skills.

Social reasons for participation

Increased leisure time

Many people take part in sporting and recreational activities who have no wish to be world champions nor even take competition too seriously. People nowadays have far more leisure time than was once the case. Many use this free time to visit health clubs, walk in the countryside and take part in any of a whole host of activities which may be available in their locality. Other opportunities are available because people are now much more mobile than ever before – a trip to the mountains or the coast, for example, is often little more than an hour or two away by car.

There are several reasons for this increase in leisure time, the most important of which are:

- the shorter working week
- technological advances
- early retirement
- unemployment.

People in the UK now have more time for leisure activities

The shorter working week

In the UK today, many workers work 37 hours per week or less. In the 1960s, a working week of between 40 and 44 hours was quite normal. Although this may not appear to be a significant reduction, for many people a saving of an hour or so per day means that it is that little bit easier to find time for recreation and leisure activities.

Additionally, the present-day statutory annual holiday entitlement of four weeks allows people to spread their holiday allowance over a considerable period. This means that a number of extended weekends can be used to accommodate sporting or recreational interests.

Technological advances

Technology has reduced the hours it used to take to do many jobs – the computer has revolutionised the world of work. To take just one example, email means that people can send documents to each other in seconds, instead of days. Technology has also made many jobs far less physically demanding than they used to be. The JCB digging holes in the road is now a common sight. At one time an army of men with shovels would have been required to do the same work.

Technological advances have not usually meant that workers now work fewer hours because they can get the same jobs done more quickly than in the past. Instead, fewer people are required to do the same job, which has caused unemployment in certain industries. However, technological advances have also created completely new kinds of work – like telephone call centres, for example. Many jobs are now more flexible, so people can adjust the hours they work to fit in leisure activities.

One big effect of technological advances has been that people are far less active in their working lives than they used to be – many workers now sit all day in front of a computer. This often makes people feel that they must do something active after work or at the weekends. This has been a big reason for the increase in participation in all kinds of sports and physical activities.

Technological advances in medicine have been enormous over the last century. People in countries like the UK are living longer, which means there are more people over the age of retirement with free time for sport and leisure activities. Advances in the media – digital TV, for example – have meant that many more people are aware of and knowledgeable about many more kinds of

sport and physical activity, which often increases participation.

Early retirement

More people now take early retirement than ever before. In some cases technological advances may have caused unemployment in their industry, or they retire because they are unwell. For others, though, it is a lifestyle decision. Work is no longer the main reason for living – they want to take some time for their own enjoyment, often to pursue leisure interests, and they can afford to do so.

Unemployment

Unemployment is when people lose or leave their jobs without having another job to go to. There are around a million people in the UK of working age who don't have a job. Unemployment gives people time to take part in sport and leisure activities (though trying to find a job can be like full time work itself), However, they may not have the money needed to do so, or, in many cases, the inclination – unemployment can be depressing and demotivating.

Technological advances have, as we saw, created large numbers of new kinds of job, and this has been, in part, the reason for there being fewer people unemployed than twenty years ago. Many of these new jobs, though, are part time or are not permanent. People in these kind of jobs do have more time and also some money (and motivation) to take part in sport and leisure activities.

The winning need not stop – nor the enjoyment of taking part

Tasks

As a group, research the leisure activities available in your community. Your local library or health centre will have some useful information. What sort of people do you think take part in each kind of activity?

Why people participate

We have just considered very briefly why many people today have more leisure time than before. While this might explain *how* sport and recreation have become more popular, it does not tell us just *why* people want to take part in physical activities at all.

As we discovered when looking at motivation in sport (page 44), there is no single answer to this – people are motivated for many different reasons. There are, however, three general categories that can help us to understand the why sport and recreation might be important to many people. These are:

- **health**
- **leisure**
- **vocation.**

These categories are fairly general and each includes a number of reasons why people participate in physical activities.

Health

People are becoming more concerned about their health and well being. Many people have stressful jobs or suffer from stress at home, and physical exercise provides a means of relaxing and reducing tension. Physical activity is also popular because it gives a sense of well-being: as you get fitter and healthier, you feel fitter and healthier and good about yourself. A programme of physical activity can also help someone to recover from illness or incapacity.

Our body image is also very important to us, and people may exercise to lose weight or tone muscle. Our society puts a lot of value on whether people look fit and active: so this can also add to the feeling of well-being.

The relatively recent rise in popularity of gymnasia and health clubs is also an indication that people are becoming much more aware of the value of regular activity, and how fitness can add to their life expectancy.

Leisure and enjoyment

Many people participate in physical activity simply because they enjoy it. Leisure activity gives us a sense of satisfaction and relaxation. It is also an opportunity to make new friends and socialise. Being part of a team can build strong friendships, and so can competing with other people! Sports clubs and societies bring people together and often have a lot of social activities as well as sporting ones.

Some recreations such as angling (one of the most popular leisure activities), cycle touring, sailing and other activities may also be hobbies. For many enthusiasts their interest in an activity occupies far more of their leisure time than the time they spend in actual participation. An activity can be a lifelong passion.

Mountain biking: one of a new generation of recreational activities

Vocation

A vocation is a job, especially a job that you are very keen to do. There are many thousands of people in the UK who take part in sport and physical activity because they work in sport or in community recreation and health. This does not just mean those who are professional sportsmen and women, but also coaches, fitness trainers, physiotherapists, recreational and sports development officers – even PE teachers!

At one time professional sport was limited to those who played soccer or rugby league, or were boxers, jockeys or one of a small number of professional golfers. Most sportspeople were amateurs: they got no money for playing or competing. Most coaches and trainers were also unpaid or, if they were professional, were paid very little and often on a part-time basis.

In the last 30 years, professional sport has grown immensely and there are now thousands of individuals in this country who earn a living from a career involved in, or with, sporting activity.

Some sports, including local league cricket, rugby league and non-league soccer, have many hundreds of part-time professionals who earn part of their living playing sport but also have full- or part-time jobs. Some are employed as sports development officers or have other sports-related careers, which allow them to have time off when they need it to play their sport. These people can be said to have semi-pro status – they are semi-professional sportspeople.

Leading sports clubs, particularly those in the major sports, also have full-time paid officers who act as secretaries, commercial managers and youth development officers, to say nothing of a whole host of administrative and support staff who work in both playing and non-playing areas of these clubs.

Jockeys were amongst the earliest professional sportsmen

This also applies to the national governing bodies of sport, and organisations such as UK Sport, Sport England and the British Olympic Association. All these bodies employ full-time staff to support their work, many of whom are enthusiasts in their own right and are also active participants in their own particular sports.

Tasks

1. Make a list of careers that are involved with sport or participation in sport.
2. From this list, choose *one* career and write a job application for it, saying why you'd like the job and what strengths you could bring to it.
3. What are the things you enjoy about taking part in sport? How many of them are *intrinsic* motivators and how many are *extrinsic* motivators (see page 44 for help on this)?

School

Promoters of physical activity

Schools play a very important part in promoting and encouraging participation in sport and physical activity. You are evidence of that yourself! In the United Kingdom they have been influential in the promotion of physical activity for centuries. In Victorian times, in particular, people thought it was very important that children took part in games. Schools have even invented games – rugby, to take one famous example, is actually named after Rugby School, where it was invented.

Today, schools influence and promote sport in a number of ways. PE lessons are the obvious example, but you will know that your teachers also do a huge amount of work providing a range of recreational and sporting opportunities after school and at the weekends. For your course, you need to know about the following ways in which schools promote participation in physical activity:

- the National Curriculum
- examination courses
- extra-curricular activities
- links with local clubs/sports providers.

The National Curriculum

The National Curriculum is created by the government and it tells state schools what subjects to teach you from the time you start primary school until the end of compulsory education when you are sixteen.

The National Curriculum has a lot of aims for PE as it is such an important subject. All pupils have to do PE from when they start school at five until the end of Year 11. This has an enormous influence on participation – think of all those children in schools across the country, taking part in games, dance, swimming, athletics, outdoor activities, and so on.

Active participation is an essential element of the subject, but PE also teaches us vital information about health, lifestyle and working with others. A good programme of physical education should provide a wide range of activity-orientated experiences designed to prepare students for a healthy and active lifestyle after they leave school. It also teaches them to be aware of and considerate to the needs of others in their communities.

School days give pupils a chance to try out different physical activities

Examination courses

Examination courses, like the one you are doing now, mean that you can get a qualification as well as enjoy taking part and learning about PE and sport. Qualifications are very important for your life after school, and examination courses in PE, Sports Science, Leisure and Tourism, etc, also encourage people to continue to take part in physical activity.

Examination courses in PE have been running for some 30 years or so, although they have changed significantly in that time. There are currently courses at GCSE and GNVQ level and you also have the opportunity to gain AS, A level, NVQ and Btech qualifications. There are also degree courses available in Physical Education and Sport as well as in Leisure and Recreation.

Examination PE is not just theoretical study. It emphasises the application of theoretical knowledge to practical situations, the value of participation. It also reinforces the work done by all students within the National Curriculum.

GCSE PE students at work

Most PE examination specifications offer the opportunity to experience adventure

One result of studying PE and sport is that you are not only participating in sport and physical activity now, but you will grow up very well informed about the issues surrounding PE, sport, recreation and the value of participation. You will be more likely to continue to take part in sport and activity after you leave school. Even further into the future, if you choose to have children of your own, you will be more likely to encourage them to take part in sport and activity.

Extra-curricular activities

Extra-curricular activities are those that take place in addition to the requirements of the National Curriculum or examination courses. Most extra-curricular activities take place out of school time – training and practices at lunchtime or after school, matches in the evenings or at weekends, courses run in holidays, and so forth.

The fact that much of this work takes place out of school time is a testament both to the enthusiasm of young people like yourself who participate, as well as the unselfish dedication of thousands of teachers who give up their free time to make these activities possible.

Extra-curricular activities commonly include:

- school sports teams
- house teams
- school clubs and societies
- expeditions and adventure activities
- skiing and sports trips abroad
- Duke of Edinburgh and Sports Leaders awards, and other award schemes
- visits to sporting events and venues.

The availability of extra-curricular activities increases interest and participation in sport and physical activity significantly.

Many students enjoy taking part in the Duke of Edinburgh award scheme

Schools can join up with local and national school sports governing bodies, which promote sport at local, district, county, national and international levels. A sport that you begin at school can take you on to competitions at district and county levels. For some individuals there will be the chance to participate in national or even international competitions.

Literally tens of thousands of young people benefit from their early experiences in school sports and recreations. These are not only personally enriching, but often ensure that sports and activities enjoyed at school will remain part of their lives for many years afterwards.

Links with local clubs and sports providers

Traditionally links between schools and local sports clubs and sports providers have been developed in a variety of ways. Teachers may be members of the clubs, or parents may be members and encourage their children to join. Joining a sports club is a great way to improve in your activity, and to meet other people who share the same interests.

Schools also often make use of off-site facilities for activities such as squash, swimming, or rock climbing. These activities require resources the school may not have itself such as squash courts, swimming pools or climbing walls. This use of other facilities may be either as extra-curricular activities or as part of National Curriculum or examination coursework requirements. All of these links can help to introduce students to a number of recreational opportunities that are not provided for in their own school or, possibly, their local community. A school expedition or a link with a local climbing club, for example, may stimulate a lifelong interest that otherwise might not have developed.

Many young people are introduced to lifelong interests while at school

It has also become more common for school facilities to be made available to local clubs, either for training or for competition, and for links to be developed as a result of this. All but the most exclusive of clubs are keen to attract young members from the local area. Even private clubs that need to make a profit encourage students to use their facilities, since these students are then be more likely to join the club when they are older.

School staff, particularly members of PE departments, often invite speakers from local clubs and associations to speak to their students. Such visits are often particularly valuable to those following examination courses or people who may also be considering careers in sport or related areas.

Speakers may include representatives of national sporting organisations, policy-making bodies such as the Sports Council and local authority sports development officers. Well-known sports personalities may reside in, or may be visiting the area and many now undertake regular programmes of school visits as part of an agreement with either their sponsors or sports funding agency.

A new network of Schools Sports Co-ordinators has recently been created. These co-ordinators will be responsible for developing links between groups of schools and outside sporting organisations.

Most Schools Sports Co-ordinators will be based in specialist sports colleges. The government aims to create over 100 specialist sports colleges by the year 2003. These will enhance links with outside sporting organisations and provide more funding for schools to develop both their own programmes of activity and those of other schools within their local networks.

All in all, schools have a very big impact on levels of participation in sport and physical activity. The support, encouragement, opportunities, facilities and links to the wider community that schools provide are all very important factors affecting participation and performance in sport and activity.

Tasks

1. What is meant by the term 'extra-curricular activities'? List the extra-curricular activities that you take part in.
2. Give *four* examples of the ways in which schools develop links with sport.
3. How many people in your group go to sports or exercise clubs outside school? Discuss this as a group and record your findings.

Social background

Positive and negative influences on participation

The right to participate in a whole range of sporting and recreational activities is taken for granted by most of us today. But there are still those who don't always have the opportunities to take part.

In the next ten pages we will look at some of the main social influences on participation in sport and activity. These influences can have a positive effect, encouraging participation, or a negative effect – they do not encourage nor limit participation. You need to know about all of them for your course. These main social influences are:

- **access**
- **age**
- **disability**
- **education**
- **environment/climate**
- **family**
- **gender**
- **media**
- **peer group**
- **politics**
- **poverty**
- **religion**
- **sponsorship**
- **tradition/culture.**

Access

Access to recreation is limited by the free time people have when they are not at work, pursuing school or college careers, or are otherwise engaged in personal or family matters that take up their time. However, for many people there is also the matter of the availability of facilities and, in many cases, the important issue of cost.

In recent years, local authorities have increased the provision of sports facilities at low cost. This has allowed a wider cross-section of people to gain access to the kind of facilities that were previously enjoyed by a relatively small and privileged group. The growth in the number of sports halls available to members of the general public, either in schools or in local or regional sports centres, has been very beneficial. Often these facilities also provide access to outdoor pitches and courts. Such facilities, which are often open until late in the evening and at weekends, allow ordinary people the opportunity to take part in regular activity.

If access to activities like this are on your doorstep, then you are very lucky!

We all have access to the countryside – or do we?

However, not everyone can take advantage of such opportunities for various reasons. Local sports centres may not have been designed to cater for the needs of all disabled people (see page 60).

For many unemployed or poorly paid people, even concessionary admission rates designed to help them might still not enable them to participate, particularly within the limits of a very tight family budget.

Swimming, for example, is a very popular activity amongst all age groups, but swimming pools and water activity centres are amongst the most expensive facilities to build and maintain. This often forces local authorities either to increase charges for admission, or to close swimming facilities or leisure centres in one area in order to keep another open elsewhere. This can limit access to those who can't afford increased prices, or who are unable or unwilling to travel to swimming centres in other areas.

Some sporting facilities are private and charge relatively high fees for membership. Membership is retricted to those who have enough money to join, and this means they have the freedom to choose not just when to take part in sport or exercise, but where as well. Access isn't an issue for them.

For others, particularly those in disadvantaged groups, access may be limited to:

- what is local
- what is available
- what is affordable.

This applies to access to the countryside, the mountains and the coast. Those who happen to be fortunate enough to live in or near these areas have access on their doorstep, as do those with enough money to be able to travel there as and when they wish. For some older people, for those who can't afford to travel and for certain other minority groups, access is not always so easy.

Age

People are living longer and are having fewer children. So older people are making up more and more of the UK's population. Over a period of time this change will be reflected in the nature of recreational activity and the provision of it.

Previously older people were not expected to take part in what were regarded as 'young people's activities'. Indeed many senior citizens themselves were convinced that certain activities at their age were either undignified or even dangerous.

Views are now changing. For a number of years, veterans' groups in many sports have grown both in number and in membership. Many older people are now fully aware of the potential benefits for health and well-being to be gained from active recreation and participate in most activity areas.

Sports that require a great deal of physical exertion will make competing at a high level difficult for older people, but for most other activities there should be no **discrimination** against them at any level.

Despite older people being more involved in a variety of sports and activities, there is still some bias against what are seen to be 'old people's sports'. Bowls is a prime example and this bias reduces involvement among younger people.

Older people themselves may be reluctant to participate in leisure activities for their own reasons. For example, they may never have done so before and may feel that they have left it too late; or simply because they may not be able to afford the fees charged by some local clubs or leisure centres.

Attitudes towards disability sport are changing

Disability

For many years, those involved in the promotion of disability sport and recreation have fought an uphill battle against a lack of provision for the particular needs of disabled people. Until recently, there has been a wide assumption that certain social groups would either not wish to, or simply not be able to take part in recreation.

The rapid explosion in participation levels in disability sport in the last two decades has proved that these views are wrong and shown how capable and determined athletes with disability are.

Disability sport is now widely accepted as 'real' sport and is seen as an exciting form of physical activity to watch and participate in. The popularity of the disability Olympic Games events in Sydney 2001 and the reception back home of the British athletes who took part is proof of this change in attitude.

> **Athletes with disability – not disabled athletes!**
> **Disability sport – not disabled sport!**

Education

Education is an important social influence on participation. As we saw on pages 54–7, school education encourages young people to take up active recreations and sports.

Most of us, whether we go on to become professional sportsmen and women or simply enjoy taking part, had our first opportunity to do so during physical education lessons, at clubs after school, or as members of house or school teams run by teachers.

Education need not, of course, stop at sixteen or eighteen. Those who go on to college or university often find a huge array of clubs and societies available that allow them to continue with those activities they already enjoy or perhaps even try some new ones.

Adult education classes, the youth service, and many other youth and adult organisations also offer continuing education, including classes in recreational and sporting activities for those who wish to improve their existing skills or learn new ones.

Education has a broader purpose than simply to encourage participation – important though that is. Education teaches people about shared responsibility and equality of opportunity. This encourages people to work towards ensuring that participation in sport and recreation is available to everyone.

Education is a strong influence on participation in sport and physical activity. Within the education system, however, there are some differences between types of schools and the resources they have available to them. Some schools are very well provided for, with lots of facilities for many different kinds of activity. Others may not have the same range of opportunities on site.

Teachers will do all they can to make sure that links with sports centres and other sports providers ensure that a large range of activities are available. However, participation in every activity area might not be possible due to limited resources in the community.

There are also other current issues, which do adversely affect the ability of schools to provide sporting and recreational opportunities and experiences, including the following:

- playing fields being sold off to raise money for other local authority projects
- a reduction of the time given to PE teachers to make way for other subjects
- schools being forced to reduce staff numbers to save money
- teachers having more administrative responsibilities and less time for extra-curricular activities.

Tasks

1. What sort of people might be affected by a decision to close a local leisure centre and open a new one ten miles away?
2. Design a poster to encourage more older people to take part in sport.
3. Research the rules and regulations of wheelchair basketball: how are they different from the rules and regulations for able-bodied basketball?
4. What are the positive and negative influences of education on participation? Give two examples of each: positive and negative.

Environment and climate

The physical (geographical) environment in which people live and the prevailing climate will have a significant effect on the kind of sports and recreations found there.

In the UK the summers are not so hot as to make outdoor activity difficult, or winters so cold that we are restricted to activity indoors. There are, of course some disadvantages to our climate, as those who have sat all day in the rain at Wimbledon or at a Test Match will know!

In some parts of the world the climate is more extreme. At certain times of the year outdoor activities can only take place if precautionary measures are taken – for example, to avoid sun-stroke. In other countries, the cold or the monsoon (rainy season) may prohibit all but the most extreme activities.

Winter sports and beach sports are examples of activities that are strongly linked to the environment and climate where they develop as popular activities. However, technology now makes it possible for some environments to be artificially created; dry ski slopes, for example, allow access to skiing in countries without the mountains and snow that is normally required.

Technology can be costly, though, and in some poorer parts of the world there is little alternative but to use the physical environment in the best way possible. Kenya in East Africa is a poor country economically, but has an abundance of both flat and high altitude terrain, ideal for marathon training.

Family

For many people their earliest experiences of sport are the games they play with family members. Parents are often interested in sport themselves and encourage their children to participate.

Parents' support and interest in the activities of their children can make an immense difference to how good young people feel about their own participation. When a parent takes little interest it is probably less likely that an interest in sport will develop unless other influences, such as school or friends, have a more positive effect.

Gender

Whether you are male or female should not make any difference to your freedom to participate in whatever sport or activity you are interested in, should it? However, the

Both of these activities are most popular where the environment supports them

long tradition of discrimination against women in sport has not completely died away, and gender does have a continuing influence on participation. Not too long ago, girls and women could not participate in a whole host of activities. This was because men thought that if women took part in sport they would hurt themselves, they would not be able to have children, and would become aggressive and competitive – i.e. not 'ladylike' – and other idiotic reasons based on keeping women under the control of men.

Women now play soccer and rugby and at long last are throwing the hammer and pole vaulting in major athletics competitions. They are no longer thought to be too frail to run 400 or 800 metres in competitive situations and have shown that they can outperform men in marathon and other ultra-endurance events. However, unfortunately many professional sports still have no organised women's events and when they do, these events are not as widely publicised as the men's events. Almost all professional sports award less prize money for women's events than for men's.

Jane Couch: champion boxer

There is still some resistance to women's participation in boxing, and Jane Couch, one of Britain's current world champions in that sport, has had to endure much abuse and criticism from all sectors of society. These criticisms usually centre on whether or not it is medically safe for women to box. Bearing in mind that there is much current debate about the safety of any form of boxing, it seems rather unfair to single out women's boxing as though it is somehow different.

Significant obstacles to women participating in sport still exist in some countries, largely because of a mixture of religious and political beliefs. This is a major issue, covered in greater depth on pages 66–7.

The media

Today high technology media exerts a greater influence than ever before upon our views of sport, recreation and related matters such as health and fitness issues.

At national and international level, television companies spend millions buying broadcasting rights to major global sporting events and want something in return for their money. They insist that events take place at certain times in order to coincide with peak viewing times – which also means that more people watch their TV commercials.

The increased competition that has arisen with the coming of satellite, digital and cable TV has meant that television companies in the UK have been in fierce bidding wars for the rights to show popular matches. Some of these rights have been lost by the five main terrestrial TV channels, and can only be seen by those with access to satellite, digital or cable TV. These non-terrestrial services have also introduced 'pay-per-view', which means people have to pay to watch a match or game. This further reduces access to sports programmes for some TV spectators.

Sport is headline news in newspapers, magazines, web sites and on television and radio. There are films about sport and a never-ending stream of sports documentaries and chat shows on television. This all gives a lot of exposure to sport and sporting issues – not all of it the sort of publicity that sports stars and managers want! However, this huge amount of sports coverage does bring it into everyone's living room and often sparks off the enthusiasm that encourages some viewers to get out there and have a go themselves.

Peer group

Peer group pressure or influence can be a major factor in the lifestyle and interests of young people. If your particular group of friends (your peers) are interested in sport then the chances are that you will be too. If this is not the case it often takes considerable strength of character to follow your own inclinations rather than just following the crowd.

Politics

In the 1960s, the western world (Europe, USA, Australasia and Japan) began to see the emergence of athletes from eastern European countries that were almost unbeatable. This success was the result of state policy. The leaders of these countries had decided that everyone should have the opportunity to play games and sports from a very early age. Every local community was given the resources to enable everyone to participate in recreation, irrespective of age. Children who showed potential were then trained very hard to become world-beating athletes.

This was done by ensuring that all children had wide programmes of training. France was the first country in western Europe to copy this approach, which includes recreational provision for everyone – not just potential champions. In Britain and many other countries, including the US, the organisation

In the 1960s, State policy in the USSR made a big impact on participation in sport

of sport developed in a rather haphazard way and was controlled by private organisations with little government intervention or funding. Even today, the provision of sports facilities is still left very much to the discretion of local councils and private organisations.

The eastern European experience shows that politics can make a big difference to participation in sport and recreation. In the UK today central government supplies local authorities with a large part of the money they have to spend on sports facilities. This money might not come directly from the government: in the UK the National Lottery funds a lot of sporting facilities and organisations. But the government sets out guidelines on who the money should go to in the first place. We are still some way from having an effective centralised organisation for sport in the UK.

Poverty

In many parts of the world people live in poverty, that is they lack the basic resources (money) needed to enjoy a full life.

If the task of feeding, clothing and finding decent shelter for a family is achieved only with great difficulty, then clearly there is nothing left to spend on those leisure activities that make life more enjoyable. This can include taking part in sport and recreational pastimes. Most people in the UK have enough to live on but it can still be difficult for some to find extra resources for recreation.

Some sports, like basketball, football and boxing, for example, do not require very expensive equipment or facilities to be played and enjoyed. Poorer areas have produced excellent football players, basketball players and boxers over the years. But this is not so much the case for sports that require expensive facilities, like swimming, golf, polo or tennis. Because facilities for such sports are not freely available, participation is not an option for those with little extra money to spare.

The Active Communities programme, sponsored by Sport England, now has a development fund that encourages deprived and ethnic minority groups to apply for funding in order to develop facilities in local areas. This development is an extension of the Active Schools programme, which provides funding for sport and PE in schools, and Active Sports. This has targeted nine of the most popular sports and provided additional funding for their development through a series of Sports Partnerships.

Sponsorship

Sponsorship is very big business in sport today. It ranges from the huge sums paid by companies for racing cars to carry their logo, to the more modest sponsorship money paid by local businesses to support local clubs. A definition of sponsorship in sport might be that it is 'the funding of sporting activity for commercial gain'.

This definition was given by the Institute of Sports Sponsorship. Founded in 1985, it is now jointly responsible with the Central Council of Physical Recreation (CCPR) for advising on sponsorship matters in the UK. Together they form the Sports Sponsorship Advisory Service, which advises Sport England, the government and potential sponsors on matters to do with this topic (see diagram below). The purpose of the Sports Sponsorship Advisory Service is to develop sport and recreation by means of commercial sponsorship.

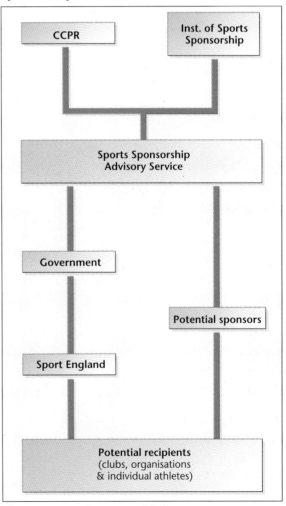

The structure of sponsorship in sport

One of the products of this relationship is called Sportsmatch, which is the government's grass-roots sports sponsorship scheme. This initiative offers to match any commercial sponsorship gained by grass-roots sports clubs or organisations, doubling the amount raised. The scheme, which began in 1992–3 has to date has handed out over £23 million to 3000 projects in 72 different sports.

Corporate (business) sponsorship also plays a significant part in encouraging participation. Funding is made available to support young sportspeople and improve facilities. In return, companies get free advertising or other benefits.

The Snickers programme provides resources to increase participation and improve performance in school soccer. By doing this, the company hopes to get more sales of its products.

Sponsorship brings its benefits but also exacts its price

Another example of corporate sponsorship is that of the company News International. It has given millions of pounds to Premier League soccer and to rugby league's Super League, in return for exclusive rights to show big matches on the satellite TV service owned by News International.

The Olympic Games uses sponsorship as a way to make the Games affordable. Its organisers have said that it could not continue to do so without the support of sponsors such as Ford and Coca-Cola™.

On the one hand, sponsorship brings much needed cash into sport, increasing participation as it does so. On the other hand, it exacts its price for doing so, putting pressure on clubs and organisations to keep their sponsors happy. A gap is also opened up between the resources available to sports and activities with a mass appeal, and those that might have more limited market.

Tradition and culture

In 1993, the Islamic Women's Games was held in Tehran in Afghanistan for the first time. Five thousand women forced their way into the stadium to watch the events. This was very much against the strict moral code of the country. The government did not think that women should mix with men at sporting activities.

In some Islamic cultures, many people think that women should not go out in public unless they cover their arms and legs, called hijab. The Algerian runner, Hassiba Boulmerka, was heavily criticised in her country for training and performing in shorts, rather than keeping her arms and legs covered.

Just because another culture or tradition is different from your own, does not mean it is wrong. There are certain international expectations regarding sport and physical activity, however, which suggest that women should be free to participate in sport on equal terms with men. Cultures which restrict the participation of women, minority (or majority) ethnic groups, or the disabled would certainly go against these international expectations, and would severely limit participation in sport and physical activity to the affected groups.

There have been occasions in the past when countries have been excluded from participation in international sporting events because of their discrimination against ethnic groups. This was the case between 1964 and 1992 when South Africa was banned from participating in the Olympic Games because the culture of the white population who ruled the country could not accept that black and white people were equal. Under the South African policy of **apartheid**, black people were not allowed to mix with white people. White people had all the power and the money, black people had almost nothing. Black people had very few opportunities at all, including in sport.

Apartheid was ended in 1992. Since then, South African sport has benefitted from participation at all levels by members of all the cultures and traditions of its population. We are lucky to live in a multicultural society in the UK, with all the richness and variety that it brings to sport.

Summary

We have seen in this chapter there are many social factors affecting participation. Many of them are to do with access – whether facilities are provided and for what activities, whether people have enough money to use them, whether or not a society thinks it is acceptable or desirable for certain groups to be allowed access, and what sort of sports are seen to be desirable or marketable. These issues are often covered in newspapers and magazines and it would benefit you to look out for these stories, cut them out and use them in your revision for the exam.

Tasks

1. Are there any sports which women should be banned from participating in? Are there any sports that men should be banned from? Discuss these questions in groups.
2. Is sponsorship good for sport? List its *advantages* and *disadvantages* as a means of encouraging participation.
3. The Socialist country of Cuba once allowed only eight sports to be played. Why do you think this was?
4. The tennis champions, Venus and Serena Williams grew up in a poor family in a poor area of New York City. Using library resources or the Internet, find out how they became champions in their sport.
5. Should we encourage participation in sport and recreation between different cultures and traditions? Why?

Growing up in a poor area of New York City has not prevented the success of Venus and Serena Williams

Local and national facilities

Provision and opportunity

On page 58–9, we saw that participation in sport often depends on access to sporting facilities. These are often expensive to build and maintain, and even if facilities exist, participation then largely depends on their being within easy reach, affordable and open at convenient times.

When thinking about participation and sporting facilities, you need to consider two key questions:

- provision – do adequate facilities exist?
- opportunity – are people able to use them?

There will always be some activities that are not easily available: skiing, for example, might require you to travel to another country to find snowy mountains. Also, some facilities may be provided specifically for the use of high-level performers who require specialised facilities.

When assessing the sort of facilities that are provided in the UK, and what effects they have on participation in sport and activity, we must look at both local provision and national provision.

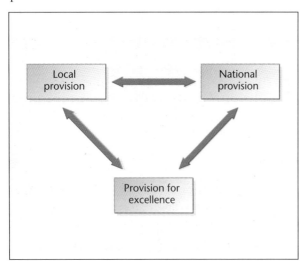

Local provision

The major providers of facilities in most localities are:

- **local authority**
- **private enterprise**
- **private and voluntary clubs and associations.**

The local authority

The main provider of facilities for most people is the local or municipal authority. This body provides and maintains:

- public parks
- public playing fields
- swimming pools
- sports facilities in schools
- local sports centres
- local youth centres.

Many of the above are used jointly by schools and local community groups in the daytime, evenings, weekends and during school holidays.

Some local authorities also fund (sometimes with outside assistance) such facilities as athletics tracks, outdoor pursuits centres and water sports centres. Youth centres are often sited within or right next to schools so that use of the recreational facilities may be maximised.

Sadly, some of these facilities have to be closed – either temporarily or sometimes permanently – when financial budgets require local authorities to make difficult choices about the range of services it can afford to maintain.

Facilities such as this are usually only found in private clubs

Private enterprise

An increasing number of recreational and sporting facilities is now offered by private health and sports clubs to those who can pay for them. These can range from squash courts and gyms to luxury health spas and private swimming pools. These enterprises operate for profit and are run as private businesses. Members normally pay a joining fee, an annual subscription and sometimes another small fee each time they use the facilities. Non-members cannot use the facilities.

Private and voluntary clubs and associations

There is a big difference between private facilities that are run as businesses to make a profit and those run by their members and which exist solely to provide playing and social facilities for them.

These non-profit making clubs and associations are usually run by elected committees. The committees work voluntarily for the good of the rest of the membership. Many local football, rugby, cricket and tennis clubs are run in this way. In some cases a full-time barperson or groundsperson is employed as well.

Both types of private club, whether profit-making or not, have the effect of providing facilities for those who can afford to pay for them. This eases the demand for facilities that are provided by local authorities and increases participation levels. However, access to these clubs is not available to people who can't afford to join.

Tasks

1. How many of the popular sports in your area are catered for by:
   a the local authority
   b private non-profit-making clubs
   c private clubs operating for profit?
2. Conduct a survey in your own school designed to identify which popular sporting facilities are not easily available.
3. How might provision for these activities be improved or created?

National provision

Like local provision, the provision of national facilities comes from a mixture of public and private funding.

At the national level, provision needs to cover a wide range of leisure activities, from top class sport at one extreme, to the need to maintain public pathways, ancient building and sites of outstanding natural beauty at the other. National provision is the responsibility of a large array of official, private and voluntary bodies such as the Countryside Agency, the Environment Agency, English Heritage and the National Trust.

For example, Twickenham, generally regarded as the home of rugby, is one of the few major venues actually owned by the sport it stages. Wembley Stadium, until recently the home of English soccer, is owned by a private company to whom the Football Association used to pay rent for internationals and major cup finals to take place there. Wimbledon, the home of the world's most prestigious tennis tournament, is owned by the All-England Club, a private organisation that stages the championship itself.

Sport England

Government-funded bodies work to organise and promote the provision of facilities both nationally and locally. In the UK there are separate sports councils for England, Wales, Scotland and Northern Ireland. The one for England is called **Sport England**.

Sport England, like the other sports councils, is concerned with encouraging participation and performance in sport and recreational activity. Part of its brief is to look at the provision of facilities and make sure they are in the right place and are working properly.

National centres of excellence

Sport England is also concerned with improving performance in national sport. It administers and maintains five national sports centres that are **centres of excellence**.

Facilities at centres of excellence are intended primarily for use by national governing bodies of sport for national and élite squad training. In some cases, such as at Holme Pierrepont and Crystal Palace, facilities are open to public groups and individuals when not required for national squad training.

The five centres in England are at:
- Crystal Palace (in London)
- Bisham Abbey (in Buckinghamshire)
- Lilleshall (in Shropshire)
- Plas y Brenin (in North Wales)
- Holme Pierrepont (in Nottinghamshire).

Crystal Palace, Bisham Abbey and Lilleshall are multi-purpose and cater for high level training in different sports. Crystal Palace also has specialist facilities for athletics, swimming and diving; Bisham Abbey has specialist tennis facilities; and Lilleshall has specialist facilities for football and gymnastics. Plas y Brenin specialises in outdoor and adventurous activities; and Holme Pierrepont in water sports.

Gymnastics facilities at the National Sports Centre, Lilleshall

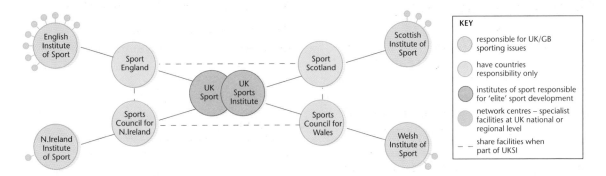

The national administration of sport in the UK

There are also specialist facilities for some sports sited outside the centres of excellence, for example swimming at the University of Bath and cycling at the new national velodrome in Manchester.

The sports councils of Scotland, Wales and Northern Ireland also fund and maintain national sports centres. Wales has Cardiff (all purpose) and Plas Menai (outdoor and adventurous). Scotland has Cumbrae (water sports), Inverclyde (all purpose) and Glenmore Lodge (outdoor and adventurous). Northern Ireland has Tollymore (outdoor and adventurous). Together, these facilities provide a network for promoting excellence in sport.

The national administration of sport

A development which came out of Soviet involvement in sport in the 1960s, 70s and 80s was its use of special schools, or institutes, which existed solely for the purpose of producing excellence in sport. These institutes provided facilities for the development of athletes, coaches, sports scientists and a host of related services.

In the 1990s, a similar administrative structure started to build up in the UK in the 1990s. It is generally believed that the poor performance of Britain's athletes at the 1996 Olympic Games in Atlanta was instrumental in restructuring the way sport is organised in the UK.

The current structure is centred upon an organisation called **UK Sport**. UK Sport is to administer the **United Kingdom Sports Institute (UKSI)**, while the sports councils of Wales, Scotland and Northern Ireland and Sport England will each look after their own sports institutes.

The English Institute of Sport is currently a network of nine regional centres. Northern Ireland, Scotland and Wales are each in the process of developing their own structures centred at Ulster, Stirling and Cardiff. When this process is complete, the network centres of each of the four home countries together with those in England will collectively form the United Kingdom Sports Institute.

The nine regional centres in England so far named (in 2001) are:

North West	Manchester (Sports City, the venue for the 2002 Commonwealth Games)
Yorkshire	Sheffield
East Midlands	Holme Pierrepont NWSC
West Midlands	Lilleshall
South East	Crystal Palace
South	Bisham Abbey
South West	Bath University
North	Gateshead
South Coast	Southampton

The tenth regional centre (**East**) has not yet been named but it is intended that the English Institute of Sport should be fully operational by the year 2002.

The current slogan on which Sport England bases its activities is:

More people, more places, more medals

This embraces both sporting and recreational concepts. While medals are important, Sport England believes it is also essential to attract as many people as possible into active participation. It supports the provision of easily accessible and affordable facilities in the places where they can be most effectively used.

Most of us like to see national teams and individual performers doing well in the international sporting arena. But are ordinary people likely to benefit from any top level success, apart from feeling proud of such performances? How will national and regional reorganisation of the way sport is provided for affect participation for those of us who aren't likely to win medals in international competition?

Gold

Elite groups

National junior squads

Teaching and coaching opportunities

Sport and recreational participation in a healthier community

The mass participation pyramid relates to the current Sport England slogan, 'more people, more places, more medals'

British success at the Sydney Olympics in 2000 was greatly helped by national lottery funding

The experiences of other countries show that sporting success is only really achievable if the top performers are chosen from a wide base of participation. The more people there are taking part in any sport, the greater the likelihood that those who rise to the top will be the best in the world. As the mass participation pyramid on the previous page shows, the bigger it is at the bottom, the higher it can be at the top.

Both UK Sport and Sport England now accept that for this to be possible the necessary funding must be targeted not only at top performers but also at grass-roots level. The Active Sports, Active Communities and Active Schools programmes (see page 65) are attempts to make sport accessible for as many people as possible. Such policies not only maximise the chances of Britain winning gold medals but also of creating a much healthier nation.

Tasks

1. Who runs the centres for excellence?
2. Why do you think the government wants more people to participate in sport and physical activity?
3. Should we be spending huge sums of money on top level performers when there is still a lack of facilities at grass-roots level? Discuss this in groups.

Components of fitness

There is no one single aspect of human performance that makes up fitness. The type of fitness required by a shot-putter and a triathlete, for example, are completely different and require very different programmes of training.

So if someone asks you 'Are you fit?', your reply should really be 'Fit for what?' before you can answer them.

There are, however, a number of **components of fitness**. They are the key to understanding what the difference is between one type of fitness and another. These components of fitness are:

- cardiovascular endurance
- muscular endurance
- speed
- strength
- flexibility.

Different components of fitness are needed in different situations

Cardiovascular endurance

Cardiovascular endurance depends on the capacity of the heart and circulatory system to meet the demands of the body for a sustained period of activity.

Cardiac output (blood pumped from the heart) is normally around five litres per minute but can rise to as much as seven or eight times that in response to the demands of a trained endurance athlete working at near to maximum level (see page 24).

Good cardiovascular endurance usually comes from long-term endurance training. It often results in an increase in the size of the heart muscles (cardiac **hypertrophy** – see page 125). It is this increase in size that allows the heart to pump a greater volume of blood carrying oxygen around the body each time it beats (Figure 1). This is particularly beneficial to those involved in activities requiring a sustained effort for an extended period of time. Look back at page 30 to remind yourself about aerobic exercise.

Figure 1 The volume of blood carrying oxygen at rest and at work

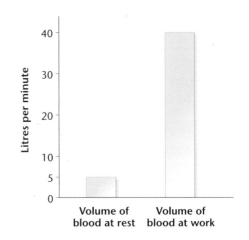

Cross-country events in the winter and both middle and longer distances on the athletics field in the summer will show which students have greater levels of cardiovascular endurance than others. Some people are born with this advantage but it can always be improved with regular and extended periods of physical activity.

Even those participating in short, explosive events benefit from some improvement in cardiovascular endurance. Increased bloodflow contributes greatly to the removal of lactic acid, which accumulates quickly in such short, frantic activities (see pages 30–1 on anaerobic exercise).

A more efficient cardio-vascular system benefits everyone, not just athletes. If the heart rate is slower, the heart does not have to work as hard to pump blood around the body and we are able to enjoy active recreations (and even run for a bus!) and feel fit and healthy, not worn out.

Using the track events in athletics as an example, Figure 2 below shows that the

endurance element of events increases as the explosive (or anaerobic) element decreases. So that while the sprinter needs very little endurance, its importance rises very rapidly in events longer than 400 metres.

Muscular endurance

Muscular endurance is a measure of the capacity of the muscles to perform repeated contractions at, or near maximum level for an extended period of time without becoming fatigued. In other words, muscular endurance is about how long your muscles can work at nearly maximum levels.

Figure 2 The realtionship between endurance and explosive events in track athletics

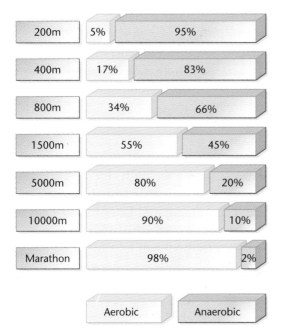

	Aerobic	Anaerobic
200m	5%	95%
400m	17%	83%
800m	34%	66%
1500m	55%	45%
5000m	80%	20%
10000m	90%	10%
Marathon	98%	2%

How long could your muscles endure this kind of position?

This type of fitness is very important in those events where power must be sustained for, say, four or five minutes, as in a 4000 or 5000 metres pursuit event in cycling or in a rowing event of 1000 or 2000 metres. Apart from the relatively short 25 metre sprint distance, most events in swimming require a considerable degree of localised muscular endurance.

In activities such as rock climbing, there are certain stretches on a pitch where there are no convenient ledges allowing a 'breather'. The muscles of the fingers, forearms and calves must be able to endure the discomfort of maintaining holds until the next secure point on the climb is reached, as in the picture on the previous page.

In activities like these, muscles have to work intensively and repeatedly for the whole event. How long muscles can work depends on the energy they can get. Once the oxygen supply fails to keep up with demand, the muscles start to work anaerobically and lactic acid accumulates (see page 22).

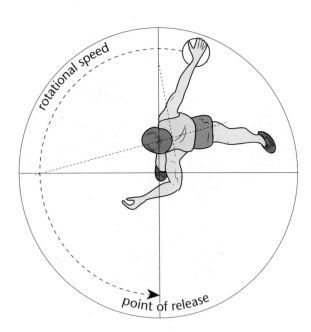

The discus thrower's speed is rotational and depends upon efficient movement

Here, muscular endurance depends on the body's lactic acid system being efficient enough to keep accumulation levels low enough to allow the muscles to continue to work.

Speed

We all tend to make the connection between speed and how fast a person can run – over 100 metres, for example. In many sports this idea of what speed means is absolutely right. For some performers, however, the speed with which other movements can be performed is also crucial. So it's important not to think of speed as always meaning running.

In the throwing events in track and field athletics, only the javelin thrower uses a run-up and this, by design, is at less than full speed. However, in each case the throwing arm must be travelling as quickly as possible at, and leading up to, the point at which the javelin, discus, hammer, etc. is finally released. Similarly, a boxer who does not work on the speedball in order to develop hand speed will be so slow to the punch that he may not get past the first round.

Many experts define speed as an innate ability, meaning we are either born with it or not. Whilst this is true, it is also true that speed can be improved with training. Most of us, even if we simply want to improve at a personal level, can develop greater leg or arm speed – even if we can never become world champions.

In many cases, speed can be improved simply by moving more efficiently. Incorrect technique that does not utilise the most efficient movement and takes longer than if it were performed correctly. In such cases, speed of movement can effectively be improved with good coaching and fault identification.

Strength

Strength is defined as:

The maximum force that can be developed within a muscle or group of muscles during a single maximal contraction.

According to this definition, strength is how much force a muscle can put out in one contraction. This refers to a very specific form of strength, which requires one all-out effort to lift a weight or throw an implement. There are other types of strength which may need to be used repeatedly, such as that required of the rugby forward involved in lots of scrums during a game; or the judo player who may make numerous attempts to throw or pin an opponent to the mat.

Almost any movement requires some strength, but for the purpose of a PE course like this, we are referring to a movement, or movements, which involve some particular effort on the part of the performer.

Most of us may not need to perform the almighty 'heave' of the shot putter or reproduce the enduring strength of the rugby forward in our everyday lives but we do require a degree of strength for many activities: sporting or otherwise.

The sedentary nature of the work that many people do in today's technological world requires little in the way of physical strength. Because our muscles quickly lose some of their strength if we don't use them, an inactive lifestyle with little or no exercise can make it much more difficult to perform tasks requiring strength, like pushing a car that won't start, or lifting heavy objects in the garden or around the house.

We need to ensure that our bodies are capable of physical strength not just for sport and physical activity, but for our everyday lives. Such considerations become even more important as we get older, as muscles naturally lose some of their strength with age. If we wish to be able to continue doing those jobs or tasks that require a degree of strength, we need to keep using our muscles on a regular basis.

Strength can be improved by regular training and exercise: especially by training with weights that push the muscles to exert their maximum force.

We often need strength when we least expect to

Some activities require numerous efforts, not just one all-out effort

Flexibility

Flexibility depends on our joints, ligaments, tendons and muscles (see page 11). Flexibility can be defined as:

The greatest range of movement possible at a given joint.

The degree of flexibility we possess is determined by several factors including the elasticity of ligaments and tendons and the strength of muscle groups.

Whilst we can define flexibility as the greatest range of movement possible *at a given joint*, as we saw on pages 8–11, not all joints allow the same amount of movement because of the difference in their construction. The ball and socket joints at the shoulder and hip, which allow movement of the arms and legs, permit the greatest range of movement. The joints of the knee and elbow permit slightly less movement, while those of the hands and feet allow even less movement.

The ways joints are constructed are the same for all of us, so that when we compare the flexibility of one person to another we must do so by comparing the range of movement *at the same joint* in each case.

As with other components of fitness, many performers require a degree of overall flexibility. This would be a part of the general conditioning programmes of most participants in most activities, at whatever level of proficiency.

Some activities (gymnastics in particular) require a degree of flexibility that can only be achieved after years of specialised and dedicated preparation.

Hurdlers need considerable flexibility at the hip joint whilst most swimmers and throwers require shoulder flexibility. All performers need to develop sufficient flexibility to allow them to perform the movements and skills necessary to their activity freely, without discomfort or fear of injury.

Most of us do not need this level of flexibility

While most people do not need to have the extreme degree of flexibility of a gymnast, we all benefit from being flexible. Reaching, bending, stretching and twisting (within reason) are all everyday movements that enable us to get the most from our normal daily lives. Flexibility also guards against tendon, ligament and muscle damage – if we slip or miss our footing, for example – so it's very important in everyday life as well as in sport and physical activity.

We are all born with a remarkable degree of flexibility but for most of us, this declines very rapidly as we get older. There is an old saying, 'If you don't use it, you lose it', and this applies as much to flexibility as it does to any other aspect of general physical activity or fitness. Inactivity is the worst enemy, and those who wish to maintain flexibility should undertake regular exercise in order to maintain it.

Flexibility can be improved by stretching exercises. Gradually extending the amount that tendons, ligaments and muscles can stretch will gradually improve flexibility.

We all need to be flexible

The components of fitness and performance

Cardiovascular endurance, muscular endurance, speed, strength and flexibility are all very important factors affecting performance. They can all be improved through training, so it follows that training to improve fitness is a good way to improve performance.

Different activities require a different balance of these components of fitness. While all activities will benefit from a good level of fitness, different activities need more of one component than others. Cardiovascular endurance is a vital factor in good performance in endurance events, while explosive strength and muscular endurance is vital in activities requiring short, all-out periods of muscular effort. Gymnastics and dance activities need more flexibility, and good performance in athletics often centres around speed.

Understanding the components of fitness required for your chosen activities gives you valuable information about how you can use training to improve your performance. We will be looking at the ways you can do this in more detail later in this book.

Tasks

1. Select *two* quite different activities (i.e. not both team games) and list the components of fitness you think are particularly important in each one. Give your reasons.
2. What is the difference between muscular strength and muscular endurance?
3. How would you differentiate between speed and agility? Give examples to support your explanation.

Skill-related fitness

The answer to the question 'How fit are you?' depends, as we saw on page 74 on 'Fit for what?'. It also depends on the kind of fitness. As well as straight physical fitness, we can also talk about **skill-related fitness**. This means fitness that affects our ability to perform particular skills.

In many activities, the way we perform physical skills is of crucial importance. In gymnastics, dance, ice skating and trampolining, a performance is marked entirely on the quality of movement and the degree to which it replicates a 'perfect model' (see page 148).

In the hammer-throw or in soccer, to take just two examples, our ability to perform skills – often when tired – is also what really counts. These aspects of fitness are said to be skill related. This means that we not only have to be fit enough to perform but fit enough to perform skilfully!

The components of fitness covered on pages 74–9 – cardiovascular endurance, muscular endurance, speed, strength and flexibility – are very important, and should not be neglected. But success in sporting (or indeed non-sporting) activity does not always rest solely upon that type of fitness.

To be successful, we need to add the following skill-related components:

- **agility**
- **balance**
- **co-ordination**
- **speed of reaction**
- **timing.**

Like the other fitness components, skill-related components can also vary in importance from one activity to another.

Agility

This involves the performer's ability to move in a controlled way and to change direction, turn, stop and start quickly. Expressions such as 'nimble' and 'quick-footed' are sometimes used to mean very much the same as 'agile'.

Agility is sometimes confused with flexibility (see page 78). But agility is not specifically to do with freedom of movement at joints but with freedom and ease of *whole body* movement.

Players in a team game may need to adjust their feet quickly in order to adopt a particular body position prior to making a tackle or a pass, or to turn quickly whilst on the move. It is the ability to adjust the position of the body quickly and in the correct way that is valuable to all participants in physical activities.

Balance

We tend to think of balance as a quality that is associated only with prodigious gymnastic feats (see below) rather than as a skill-related fitness component. As with most other skill-related components it is an important aspect of almost any physical activity.

The balance beam: most of us need to balance at a more down-to-earth level

In many sports and games, the concept of balance relates to our ability to keep our centre of mass (the bulk of our bodyweight) over our base of support. A tennis player must be able to move in any direction in order to return an opponent's shot and must therefore be in a balanced position to do so.

A sense of balance implies a sense of control. If you need to stretch to reach or catch a ball, the position of your feet are automatically adjusted in order to avoid the body mass getting outside the base of support (overbalancing).

This ability to control and adjust body position is a necessity in our everyday lives. In most instances we do it without conscious thought: such as in reaching for something from a high shelf or in turning quickly when someone calls us from behind.

Co-ordination

Co-ordination occurs as a result of interaction between the body's motor (movement) system and the nervous system. It enables the various parts of the body to combine in producing a desired movement or sequence of movements.

The ability to produce co-ordinated movement is necessary for the successful performance of sporting skills. Co-ordination is essential in maintaining balance and controlling the movement of limbs as they play their separate parts in throwing or passing, kicking, catching or striking a ball, or in avoiding, dodging or sidestepping an opponent.

In any of the movements above, each part of the body must move in a particular way, at a specific time, if the skill or movement is to be performed successfully and efficiently.

Co-ordination enables us to combine body movements

In sprinting, speed of reaction is vital

As with the other skill-related components, co-ordination is something we are born with and some people are naturally more co-ordinated than others. It can however, be improved with practice. In many cases this can be achieved by practising the skills that are involved in the sport or range of activities concerned.

Speed of reaction

The speed with which we react to a given situation can be crucial: both in sport and in everyday life. With a quick response a small, valuable object falling from a shelf may be caught before it smashes on the ground; a shot flying towards the top corner of the goal may be saved; or a sprinter may react more quickly to the gun than others in the race and be first away from the blocks.

Although the precise nature of the responses in each case will be different, the mechanisms involved are the same and essentially involve two closely related processes:

- **reaction time**
- **movement time**.

Reaction time is the time it takes between the initial stimulus (e.g. the ball is seen to be kicked towards the goal) and the initiation of a response on the part of the goalkeeper (he starts to move to stop the ball).

Movement time is the time taken between the initiation of a response and the completion of the movement. So, it's the time taken between the goalkeeper deciding on the right move to save the goal and his starting to move (initiation of the response) and making the save itself (completion of the movement).

Response time – the speed of reaction – is the total amount of time between the initial stimulus, the response to it and the completion of that response, so that:

$$\begin{aligned} & \text{reaction time} \\ + \; & \text{movement time} \\ = \; & \text{response time} \end{aligned}$$

Timing

This is not always to do with speed. In many cases it is simply about performing a skill at the right time or in the right way so that it is effective. The timing of a pass in rugby or soccer can be crucial, just as the success of a stroke in cricket depends quite considerably on it being executed at the right time.

Timing can be influenced by internal mechanisms (e.g. spotting the landing from a somersault) or, as in the examples given above, the degree to which we can relate to and respond to what others are doing in a game.

Improving skill-related components of fitness

Agility, balance, co-ordination, speed of reaction and timing – the skill-related components of fitness – are all very important factors affecting performance, so we need to know if we can improve them to better our performance. Also, different activities might require more of a particular skill-related component than others, so we need to improve especially components that most affect performance in our chosen activities.

Because skill-related components are largely to do with the control of the nervous system,

they are more difficult to improve than the more 'physical' components of cardiovascular endurance, muscular endurance, speed, strength and flexibility. The nervous system is controlled by the brain. The brain sends signals to the muscles through the nerves to tell the muscles to move, and what way to move in. How fast the brain can get its messages to the muscles is therefore important in how quickly we can twist and turn, how fast we can react to a change in balance, whether we will move our hand to the right place in order to catch a ball, how fast we react and how well we can read a game or situation.

How fast messages travel down the nerves and how fast the muscles react is not something we can directly improve by training. People born with a high proportion of fast twitch muscle fibres (see page 13) will have quicker reaction times than those with a lower proportion. This is a natural ability and something you can't change.

However, the great thing about the brain is that it *learns*. The more you practise skills and take part in your activities, the better your brain becomes at anticipating what you will need to do next.

Improving the physical components of fitness (see page 74), such as strength or speed, also lays the foundation for improving the skill-related ones through practice and training.

Tasks

1. Why is it that skill related fitness components are not as readily improved by training as purely physical ones?
2. Give *three* examples from different activities illustrating the importance of balance in sports.
3. How would you differentiate between speed of reaction and timing?

Factors affecting fitness

A healthy diet

We need food for thee reasons:

- **growth**
- **energy**
- **tissue replacement and repair.**

Some foods are good for us whilst others are not. A balanced, **healthy diet** is one that provides us with the nutrients we need and does not lead to ill health – often simply because we eat too much of a particular food group, such as sugars or fats. A balanced diet has seven essential components: carbohydrates, protein, fats, minerals, vitamins, fibre and water (see Figure 3).

Carbohydrates

Carbohydrates are high in glucose (energy) and are stored in the liver and kidneys. They are the most readily available form of energy, not just for sports performance but for everyday life.

Energy can be stored in the body in the form of carbohydrate and this is particularly important for endurance performers, who may not be able to restock their energy stores adequately while they are competing. Marathon runners often eat large amounts of carbohydrate-rich food, like pasta, in the period leading up to a competition. This practice is commonly referred to as carbo-loading.

Protein

Protein supplies about ten per cent of the body's energy requirements but is also important for growing new tissue in the body. It also contributes to the development and growth of hormones and haemoglobin in the blood (see page 28), both of which are essential for those involved in sport or regular physical activity.

Fats

There are many forms of fat in the body and it supplies around 70 per cent of our energy requirements. Although fat is the body's preferred energy source it also uses energy in the form of stored carbohydrate (glycogen) for intensive bursts of energy .

Figure 3 The components of a balanced diet

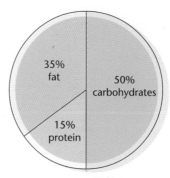

35% fat

50% carbohydrates

15% protein

Suggested energy mix for the UK diet (excluding alcohol)

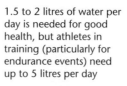
1.5 to 2 litres of water per day is needed for good health, but athletes in training (particularly for endurance events) need up to 5 litres per day

30 grammes of fibre per day will keep food moving through the gut

Minute quantities of vitamins and trace elements of minerals are needed in the diet

If we consume an excessive amount of fat it is stored in the body tissues and causes us to become overweight. In order to avoid this risk, dieticians recommend that we should not consume more than one third of our daily nutritional needs in the form of fat.

Minerals

Minerals are required by the body for building tissue. The most common ones are:

- calcium – forms bones and teeth
- sodium – regulates body fluids
- iron – helps in the transport of oxygen by red blood cells
- iodine – used in hormone formation.

Vitamins

Vitamins are chemical compounds found in the food we eat and they occur in two main groups:

- fat soluble vitamins – vitamins A, D, E and K
- water soluble vitamins – vitamins B and C.

Vitamins are important to the normal functioning of the body and this is especially so for those involved in regular physical activity. Vitamins perform the following functions. They:

- aid growth
- increase resistance to infection
- regulate some body functions
- help the metabolism of certain foods.

Vitamins are also needed to prevent certain deficiencies. A low vitamin intake can cause deficiencies in eyesight and bone growth, both of which are common in poorer countries.

Fibre

Fibre regulates the digestive system and is found (as cellulose) in fruit and in vegetables.

Fibre helps to retain water in the intestinal tract and is an important component in the removal of waste products as faeces.

Water

Water makes up more than 70 per cent of the human body – we are mostly water! It helps remove unabsorbed food and other waste products and is essential for the body's chemical reactions, all of which need to take place in water. Water is an essential part of blood, which carries oxygen and nutrients around the body.

Water is also essential in stopping us overheating. The water in our body absorbs the heat we produce when we exercise and we then lose this heat by sweating. When we sweat, the heat is carried to the surface of the skin and lost as the sweat evaporates into the air.

The downside of this very effective process is that we lose water as we exercise, which is why it's very important to replace this water to prevent **dehydration**. If the body gets too hot and too short of water, it has to stop moving, which is what happens with heat exhaustion.

Tasks

1. What are the seven components of a balanced diet?
2. From what you know about aerobic exercise, why would marathon runners stock up on carbohydrates?
3. Do you eat a balanced diet? Check the packaging of the food you eat in one day and list the amounts of the seven essential components each food contains. Which component do you eat most of and which the least? How does this compare with the balanced diet pie chart shown on the opposite page?

Physical differences

Physique means the way a body is put together – our body type. The human race contains people with a wide range of physical characteristics. Some of us are large while others are small; some of us are short and other are tall. Some people possess what is commonly referred to as 'an athletic build'. Differences in physique can have an effect on fitness, and in some cases on our health.

It is true that for certain sporting activities, a particular body type is advantageous. The diminutive gymnast, the huge shot-putter and the lanky basketball player are examples of this. Fortunately, many sports and recreations can (and do) accommodate a wide range of physical attributes.

Apart from height, it is in body type that the most obvious physical differences are evident. These body types are classified into three groups:

- ectomorph
- endomorph
- mesomorph.

Ectomorph

An ectomorph is a very slightly built person, possessing very narrow shoulders and hips and usually (but not always) long limbs, making them quite tall. Ectomorphs are often referred to as 'skinny', but this can be rather misleading as many are quite well developed muscularly.

Endomorph

Endomorphs are typically (and often cruelly) referred to as possessing a round or 'pear-drop' shape. They normally have narrow shoulders but broad hips and usually carry weight both around their waist and on their hips and upper thighs. The image of the extreme endomorph is probably best illustrated by the sumo wrestler. In sumo wrestling, sheer body mass is crucially important.

Mesomorph

The mesomorph body type represents the typical 'athletic build'. A mesomorph has broad shoulders, narrow hips and is muscular. This body type is often referred to as an 'inverted triangle' – in many ways the exact opposite of the endomorph. Many gymnasts, although they may not be tall, have a typical mesomorphic body build. This is largely due to the effects of both training and competition on the upon upper body development.

Which somatotype?

We all possess some aspects of each of these characteristics in our physical make-up, but in varying degrees. Very few people are pure ectomorphs, endomorphs or mesomorphs. We are usually a bit more of one or two types than of another.

The three body types are like the three points of a triangle, as in the diagram here. In the middle of this triangle would be someone who has a body type with equal amounts of ectomorphy, endomorphy and mesomorphy. Most of us would appear somewhere in or around the circle shown in the centre.

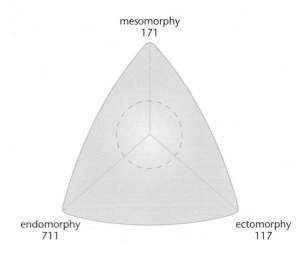

mesomorphy
171

endomorphy
711

ectomorphy
117

A classic mesomorph

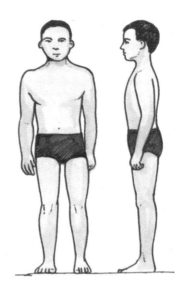

A classic ectomorph

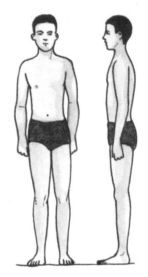

A classic endomorph

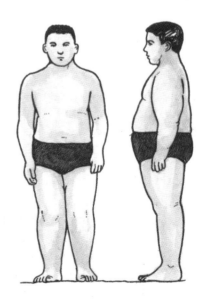

How do we know what body type we have? There is a series of tests that can be done to work out your **somatotype**, which is the term for the accurate determination of body type. Measurements are taken of height and weight, body fat, bone width and muscle girth. These measurements give a score which tells you where your body type is in relation to the three points of the 'triangle': endomorph, ectomorph and mesomorph (see page 86).

The results might indicate you to be an ectomorphic mesomorph, for example, which would mean you had your highest rating in height and thinness, and your second highest rating in muscle.

In certain sports, some somatotypes are a positive factor in success. Sumo wrestlers need to have a strong endomorphic tendency in their body type. In athletics, sprinters benefit from the muscle power of a more mesomorphic body type, while a high-jumper, where height and body weight are crucial factors, would benefit from a more ectomorphic somatotype.

Height

Clearly, tall (ectomorphic) people will have a distinct advantage when playing basketball, or competing in the high jump event. They may also gain advantage in hurdles events, as long as their height does not give them such a long stride that they find it difficult to fit in the strides between the hurdles.

In gymnastics, tall people might find that their limbs are so long that it is difficult to control them when performing particularly agile and complex moves. The advantage gained by tall people on the basketball court might well become a disadvantage when playing games in which the ball stays much nearer to the ground. Here, mesomorphic and endomorphic somatotypes may have a built-in advantage.

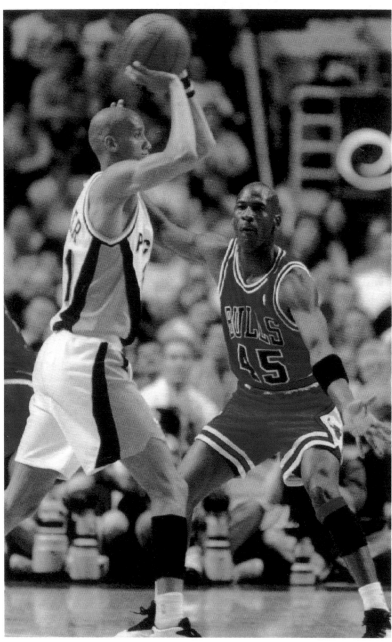

Height is an advantage in basketball

Weight

The influence of bodyweight is perhaps rather more obvious – particularly if it is excessive. Mobility and speed may well be adversely affected and people who are seriously overweight will almost certainly find it difficult to sustain activity for the whole duration of a team game, for example.

There are power based sports, such as weightlifting, where, in some classes, huge bodyweight confers a distinct advantage. Sumo wrestling, again, is perhaps the most obvious example of excessive bodyweight being deliberately encouraged.

Weight and health

Being the wrong weight can lead to some health problems. The risk of heart attacks, strokes and high blood pressure increases for people who are overweight.

Guidelines on weight measure height as well as weight, to try to take into account the differences between physique (body type). Figure 4 on the right gives general guidelines for a healthy weight range for different heights. These guidelines are designed for adults; it is important to remember that people like you are still growing and developing physically.

This sort of table is not a very accurate way to assess the relationship between weight and health. We know that different somatotypes will have different bodyweights, for example, but does that mean that a superfit, heavily muscled, 16 stone prop forward is less healthy than a 12 stone couch potato?

A more accurate measure comes from measuring not weight but the percentage of body fat. As a general rule body fat should represent no more than 20 per cent of bodyweight for men and 30 per cent for women. Again, though, this is guideline for adults.

Figure 4 Guidelines on weight in relationship to height in adults

Height	Males		Females	
Metres	kg	lbs	kg	lbs
1.54	...	...	44–57	97–125
1.56	...	...	45–58	99–127
1.58	51–64	112–141	46–59	101–130
1.60	52–65	114–143	48–61	105–134
1.62	53–66	116–145	49–62	108–136
1.64	54–67	119–147	50–64	110–141
1.66	55–69	121–152	51–65	112–143
1.68	56–71	123–156	52–66	114–145
1.70	58–73	127–160	53–67	116–147
1.72	59–74	130–163	55–69	121–152
1.74	60–75	132–165	56–70	123–154
1.76	62–77	136–169	58–72	127–158
1.78	64–79	141–174	59–74	130–163
1.80	65–80	143–176	...	...
1.82	66–82	145–180	...	...
1.84	67–84	147–185	...	...
1.86	69–86	152–189	...	...
1.88	71–88	156–194	...	...
1.90	73–90	160–198	...	...
1.92	75–93	165–205	...	...

Tasks

1 What is measured to work out somatotype?
2 For any *three* sports or activities you like, list a physical characteristic that would be an advantage for performers in those activities.
3 Why might tall people find themselves at a distinct disadvantage in some sports? Give examples to support your answer.

Age, gender and disability

Age, **gender** (whether we are male or female) and **disability** can all affect the components of fitness (see page 74). Age, gender and disability can each have an influence upon our participation in recreation, in sport and in life generally.

Age

The ageing process affects us all. As we get older, our bodies slow down so that we can no longer do many of the things we could do when we were younger; or at least not quite as well – or as quickly. Muscles, including the heart, lose some of their capacity for long endurance and for effort, so that endurance and strength are reduced. We also become less flexible with age. But all these effects can be reduced by continuing to take part in physical activity throughout life. This has an enormously beneficial effect on both fitness and health.

Bones become more brittle with age. Although endurance levels can be maintained quite effectively with regular activity, the level of dynamic strength and the capacity of the body to withstand the substantial impact involved in contact activities does decline. Reaction speed and limb speed also both reduce. Although this can be prolonged by continued activity it is usually advisable for older people to reduce their participation in heavy contact sports and replace it with a less high contact activity.

The number of older people now competing regularly in marathons and half marathons seems to bear this out and most medical opinion seems to support the notion that this type of activity combined with regular flexibility exercise is an excellent way of maintaining good health.

Gender

There are differences in the physical capabilities of males and females. Men are naturally more muscular than women, which affects strength. There can be significant differences in performance between men and women in events that call on a high degree of strength, explosive power and speed.

On average, women have a 30 per cent greater fat content than men and it is thought that this contributes greatly to their muscular endurance. As we know, strength and endurance are both components of fitness that can be improved through training. In endurance events in particular, there is little difference in performance between men and women.

As women get older, changes in their hormonal systems can make their bones more brittle, which can affect performance. Advances in medical science have produced drugs that drastically reduce such symptoms. Physical exercise also helps to maintain bone density.

Social attitudes (see pages 62–3) have been much more important than physical differences in affecting participation and performance in different sports and activities on the basis of gender. It may well be that

It is important to stay flexible as you get older

Women's rugby: this is now gaining wider acceptance but only relatively recently

social limitations rather than physical ones have prevented women from performing on a par with men in many activities. The same applies to men for activities like dance and gymnastics, which used to be thought of by some as being unmanly.

Disability

There are many different kinds of disability. As we get older, we will all become less mobile; our vision is likely to become less acute; we will all become less able at things we could do easily when younger. There are also people who become physically or mentally less able through inherited conditions, illnesses and accidents.

Some specific conditions affect certain components of fitness. Arthritis, for example, is a disability that can affect people at any age, though it is more common in older people. This disease causes inflammation of the joints and makes movement very painful. Developments in medicine have made some difference to these conditions.

Modern technology now makes participation possible for some people who could not previously enjoy active recreations because of various forms of disability. Newly developed aids such as wheelchairs and prostheses can

also improve the quality of participation for those who already take part in sport.

The components of fitness are as important for disability athletes as for any other sportspeople. They all rely on training to improve the same physical and skill-related components of fitness. It is very important to clarify the type of disability when discussing the effects it can have on the different components of fitness.

The physical components of fitness are all affected by age. Some of them, such as strength and stamina, differ between the sexes and they can be affected by disability. But all these components of fitness can either be improved, or their decline reduced, with regular practice or training.

Tasks

1. Why might older people want to stay fit?
2. Why would a higher proportion of body fat make women better designed for endurance events?
3. Do some research on how wheelchair athletes train. You could use the internet for this, if you have access to it. You should look at training to improve physical fitness, and training to improve skill related fitness.

Lifestyle influences

We are all affected to a greater or lesser degree, by what we see going on around us each day. The fact that we are so easily influenced by other people's lifestyles is why huge fortunes are made by advertising agencies. Some of these influences are in fact potentially harmful, and can have a seriously bad effect on our level of fitness

For your course you need to know about the following factors affecting fitness:

- **smoking**
- **alcohol**
- **eating disorders**
- **drugs**
- **stress.**

All of these factors may be harmful in one or both of the following ways:

- they can damage our health
- they can have a negative effect on sporting performance or on a sport as a whole (cheating).

Smoking

The view on smoking has changed drastically in the last twenty years or so. At one time most people thought it was a 'cool' thing to do, with widespread advertising by tobacco companies in the press and on television. Then it was confirmed that smoking has appalling effects on health. We are all now aware of the harmful effects of tobacco and know that smoking cannot be a part of a healthy lifestyle.

One hundred and twenty thousand people die every year from smoking-related diseases. But there are still around 450 young people taking up smoking every day in the UK (see Figure 5).

Figure 5 Smoking as a percentage of the 16-year-old population: 1992–99

Year	1992	1994	1996	1998	1999
Boys	9%	10%	11%	9%	8%
Girls	10%	13%	15%	12%	10%
Total	10%	12%	13%	11%	9%

Young people often think that people only die from smoking when they're old and that smoking won't affect them. But in fact it is harmful at any age, and has serious consequences for the components of fitness. Smoking:

- increases the likelihood of heart malfunction
- increases the likelihood of blockages in the veins and arteries
- causes damage to and reduces the capacity and efficiency of the lungs
- reduces the oxygen-carrying capacity of the blood
- negatively affects the process of gaseous exchange.

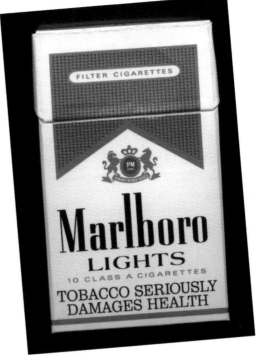

And smokers don't just do this to themselves. Passive smoking, or inhaling smoke from someone else's cigarette, means that other people who care about their health can still suffer from the same effects.

Alcohol

Drinking alcohol is a socially accepted activity. In the UK, drinking is a part of many social activities. A small amount of alcohol each week is sometimes recommended for older people, as it has some health benefits. But excessive drinking has very serious consequences for health. Alcohol can also have a negative effect on performance in sport and physical activity.

Alcohol is associated with the relaxing social side of sport and in moderation it's an enjoyable aspect of most people's lives.

Some performers have battled to fight an addiction to alcohol

Because of the negative effects alcohol has on co-ordination, balance and agility, drinking takes place after an event or match, never before! There are sports where alcohol has been used to unfair advantage. Its consumption is banned in sports such as pistol shooting, archery, fencing and modern pentathlon, because a small amounts of alcohol reduces stress and steady a shaking hand.

Alcohol is a **diuretic** drug, which means that it increases the loss of fluid through urination. Since water is so essential to performance, this is obviously something performers wish to avoid.

Alcohol also slows down reaction time and may lead to unjustified confidence in ability or a misguided assessment of a situation – these are the reasons why it is illegal to drink and drive. These effects could lead performers to believe they are capable of working beyond their safe limits.

Eating disorders

Eating disorders are illnesses that make people binge or starve themselves because of a compulsion to be thin. Eating disorders can have a very serious effect on general health and well-being. They will also affect performance in sport.

The most common types of eating disorder are:

- **anorexia nervosa**
- **bulimia nervosa**
- **compulsive eating disorder.**

Anorexia nervosa
Anorexia is a kind of self-imposed starvation. Anorexics are obsessed with their appearance, imagining that they are too fat.

Bulimia nervosa

Bulimia refers to uncontrolled eating and to related thoughts, behaviours and a poor self-image. Binge eating is usually followed by feelings of self-disgust and vomiting.

Sufferers from both anorexia nervosa and bulimia nervosa become obsessed by their weight and their image of themselves. They often involve themselves in vigorous exercise as an attempt to control their weight and improve their image. Colleges in the USA currently report that between 10 per cent and 30 per cent of their women's athletic teams have eating disorders. This is not uncommon in women's sports generally.

In a sporting environment, there is an emphasis on body size – particularly for women – that is even greater than in society as a whole. Size and shape are seen as not only reflections of femininity but also as necessary for sporting success.

There is therefore felt to be a particular relationship between sport and eating disorders. Some sportspeople use their sporting role as a justification for excessive thinness. There are some sports where this is more likely to be the case, for example, gymnastics, distance running, horse racing, figure skating, dancing and body building. In the USA, cheerleaders are also known to be amongst the high-risk groups.

The high incidence of sportspeople who suffer from chronic eating disorders has given rise to the term 'athletica nervosa', referring to those whose eating disorder is strongly connected with a need to exercise.

Compulsive eating disorder

This usually takes the form of episodes of uncontrollable over-eating. It is thought that 20 per cent of people suffering from obesity have significant problems with binge over-eating. People who have compulsive eating disorder do not normally make themselves vomit after eating or become obsessed with exercise.

Tasks

1. Why do you think that many young people are still tempted to take up smoking, despite the clear indications that it is damaging to health?
2. Explore why under-eating would have a negative effect on performance.
3. Tobacco advertising is now banned or discouraged at some sporting venues. Should this also apply to alcohol? Discuss this question in groups.

There is pressure in some sports for performers to be thin

Performance enhancing drugs

Performance enhancing drugs, as the name suggests, are drugs that can improve performance. The use of drugs in sport is not a new issue: there is evidence that athletes were taking substances to improve performance 2000 years ago in the first Olympic Games in Ancient Greece. The first drug tests in the modern Olympics were at Munich in 1972 – ironically in the former East Germany where much of the abuse of drugs was taking place at this time.

Performance enhancing drugs are taken, usually knowingly, with the intention of gaining unfair advantage over one's opponents. They include:

- **stimulants** – e.g. amphetamines
- **narcotic analgesics** – painkillers
- **anabolic steroids** – e.g. Stanazol
- **diuretics** – used to rid the body of fluid
- **other hormones** – e.g. human growth hormone (hgh)
- **erythropoietin (EPO)** – used to stimulate red blood cell production
- **beta-blockers.**

Stimulants
The most commonly used stimulants are amphetamines, which reduce the effects of tiredness and increase feelings of aggression/competitiveness. They are normally associated with the longer endurance events such as cycling and long distance swimming.

Narcotic analgesics
These are painkillers and are often used by athletes and sports performers to mask the pain of injury. This is a dangerous practice as it can result in injuries becoming even more serious than before. After all, pain is the body's way of telling us to stop something.

Anabolic steroids
These are artificial substances, which have the same effect as substances that occur naturally in the body (e.g. testosterone). Anabolic steroids do not build muscle bulk by themselves, as most people think. They do, however, permit the body to recover from heavy training loads much more quickly than would normally be possible. This means that more training can be done more quickly.

If steroids are taken in large enough doses, they can allow training to produce rapid muscle development at a rate that is not normally possible. They are now known to cause dangerous long-term side effects, which are very harmful to health.

Diuretics
These drugs are used to expel water from the body at an accelerated rate. They are particularly common in sports like horse racing where a jockey's bodyweight is critically important. Diuretics are also taken in sports where bodyweight is not critical because they are known to mask the presence of other performance enhancing substances.

Ben Johnson: still the most well-publicised instance of steroid abuse

Erythropoietin

Better known by its abbreviated name of EPO, this drug is largely undetectable because the body dilutes it within 72 hours. It has the effect of greatly increasing the production of red blood cells, which as carriers of oxygen to the muscles can produce significant benefits in endurance events.

Beta-blockers

Many substances are not in themselves illegal – they are available to the general public on prescription – but are banned for athletes in competition because they unfairly enhance performance. Beta-blockers are an example of this. Their purpose is to slow down or regulate the heartbeat in persons with heart problems but when used in sports like pistol-shooting or archery they can be used to gain unfair advantage because they reduce hand-shake.

Blood doping

Blood doping involves the intravenous infusion of blood into an athlete's bloodstream in order to increase the blood's oxygen-carrying capacity.

Blood is usually withdrawn from the athlete several weeks before a major competition. The red blood cells are extracted before the remaining components of blood are immediately re-injected to allow the body to rebuild its missing red cells.

A few days prior to the competition the original red cells are then re-injected with the result that the body's red blood cell count may be increased by up to 20 per cent above normal levels. Because the blood is the athlete's own, it is very difficult to detect that this form of cheating is going on.

Stress

Stress (or anxiety) and arousal can act as both motivators and depressors of performance levels (see pages 44–7). Either, or both, in moderate amounts can act as a spur to better performance. At the opposite extreme, too much stress can seriously reduce the ability of a performer to produce anything like his or her best form. Over-arousal can have very much the same effect.

Stress levels can be managed in any of the following ways:

- setting easy targets to begin with (lower weights in a weightlifting competition)
- mental rehearsal and positive imagery (visualisation of success – see page 45)
- verbal reassurance from coach and/or supporters
- relaxation – both physical and mental – in order to reduce stress levels.

Beta-blockers are banned in this sport because they give unfair advantage

It is quite normal to experience a certain amount of stress or anxiety prior to a competition. This only becomes a problem when the level of stress inhibits performance.

Stress can be a big problem outside sport as well, affecting people's everyday lives. Pressures at school, at work, and within the family, can all become a real problem. Medical opinion now recognises that stress can reduce the body's ability to fight infection. Taking part in sport and activity is one very good way to reduce stress in everyday life.

Arousal – being keyed up – is more associated with motivation (see page 47). Like stress, it is beneficial in moderate amounts. Arousal is necessary in sport: to perform at a high level arousal needs to be at an optimal level. When arousal is rewarded by good performance it continues to be an asset to the performer. However, if mistakes occur in performance, arousal can be accelerated and simply become stress (see Figure 6).

Figure 6 The positive and negative effect of arousal on performance

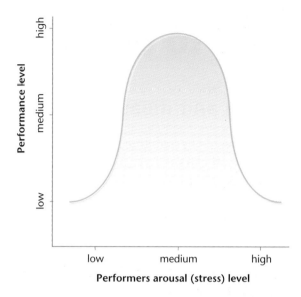

Over-arousal acts negatively upon performance levels and in this way both stress and arousal can result in performance that is way below normal levels.

Negative responses from a crowd or audience can cause over-arousal in some performers and raise stress levels in others. Sometimes, the 'big occasion' will get to a player so that they either becoms too stressed to compete well or so over-aroused that the resultant loss of control has much the same result.

Arousal rewarded by good performance is an asset

Tasks

1 Explain why might athletes want to increase the oxygen-carrying capacity of their blood?
2 Research the harmful effects performance enhancing drugs can have on health.
3 If a professional athlete is banned for life as a result of being found guilty of drug-taking, this means that effectively they are barred from pursuing their profession. Is this justifiable? Discuss in groups.

Investigation of the effect of fitness on performance and how to assess it

Testing and measurement

Testing a range of capabilities can be useful in two ways. It can measure progress in a specific aspect of fitness and can also help identify those who naturally possess particular abilities. The OCR specification requires you to be familiar with seven such tests:

- the multistage fitness test
- the 12-minute run
- sprint tests
- sit and reach test
- press-ups/sit-ups
- agility run test
- stork stand test.

The multistage fitness test

The multistage fitness test measures cardiovascular endurance (see pages 74–5). Although it is not performed under strict laboratory conditions, this test (also known as the bleep test) is a fairly accurate estimate of an athlete's **VO$_2$ max**. It is useful as a convenient means of testing large groups of people.

VO$_2$ max is the maximum amount of oxygen (in millilitres) that we are able to use in one minute for every kilogram of our bodyweight. In other words, it is a measure of how efficiently our heart and lungs can get oxygen to our muscles over a period of time.

The test is performed by running up and down a 20-metre course. At each end there is a marker such as a cone. Performers time their runs so that they coincide with an electronic bleep at each end of the course. Because of the repeated stops and turns it is very appropriate for games players though not ideal for cyclists or others whose events require continuous steady activity.

The test has 21 levels, each of which lasts for one minute and consists of a series of 20-metre shuttles. The number of shuttles increases at each level so that running speed also gets gradually faster.

When the athlete feels that he or she can no longer continue, the level and the number of shuttles completed are recorded and the test tables are consulted in order to arrive at a VO$_2$ max score.

The multistage fitness test measures cardiovascular endurance

You can measure progress in your cardiovascular endurance by running the multistage fitness test at regular times in your training programme, and comparing the most recent score with previous ones. However, it is important to understand that improvements will not occur simply by repeatedly taking the test. You will have to do some form of regular aerobic training between tests to improve.

This test might also be used to identify people who naturally possess a high endurance capacity. The results could be used to indicate whether these people might be suited to particular activities, such as middle and long distance running or cycling, where good cardiovascular endurance is an important factor affecting performance. Figure 7 at the bottom of this page shows typical VO_2 max results for top male and female performers in selected sports.

This test needs to be carried out with some caution, as it encourages participants to continue until they can run no further for results to be meaningful. Your teacher should

Figure 8 Multistage fitness test results in terms of VO_2 max – selected scores

Level	Shuttle	VO_2 max	Level	Shuttle	VO_2 max
6	2	33.6	7	2	37.1
6	4	34.3	7	4	37.8
6	6	35.0	7	6	38.5
6	8	35.7	7	8	39.2
6	10	36.4	7	10	39.9

Level	Shuttle	VO_2 max	Level	Shuttle	VO_2 max
10	2	47.4	11	2	50.8
10	4	48.0	11	4	51.4
10	6	48.7	11	6	51.9
10	8	49.3	11	8	52.5
10	11	50.2	11	10	53.1
–	–	–	11	12	53.7

Level	Shuttle	VO_2 max	Level	Shuttle	VO_2 max
14	2	61.1	15	2	64.6
14	4	61.7	15	4	65.1
14	6	62.2	15	6	65.6
14	8	62.7	15	8	66.2
14	10	63.2	15	10	66.7
14	13	64.0	15	13	67.5

Figure 7 VO_2 max figures for selected sports

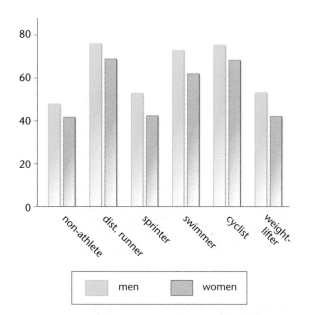

check out the BAALPE publication *Safe Practice in Physical Education* for guidance on this test.

Figure 8 above gives some indication of what results in the multistage fitness test mean in terms of VO_2 max. Only selected levels are shown. So, for example, the VO_2 max result for someone completing level 15 of the multistage fitness test (10 shuttles) would be 66.7: an indication of good cardiovascular endurance.

The 12-minute run

The **12-minute run test** is also a good indicator of aerobic capacity and cardiovascular endurance. As with the multistage fitness test, it can be used as a reasonably accurate guide to VO_2 max capacity.

Ideally, it should be performed on a 400-metre athletics track, simply because it is flat and smooth, but the required distance can be marked out on a sufficiently large hard surface area or on a playing field. Cones or other markers are placed at 100-metre intervals and the aim is to complete as many 400-metre circuits plus 100-metre intervals as possible within the time limit of 12 minutes.

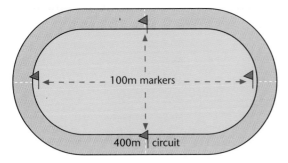

A course for a 12-minute run

By adding the number of 400-metre circuits to the number of 100-metre intervals during the final lap, a total distance for the twelve-minute period can be calculated.

Figure 9 12-minute run test tables (younger athletes)

Age	Exc	Ave+	Ave	Ave-	Poor
Male 13–14	2700+	2400– 2700	2200– 2399	2100– 2199	< 2100
Fem. 13–14	2000+	1900– 2000	1600– 1899	1500– 1599	< 1500
Male 15–16	2800+	2500– 2800	2300– 2499	2200– 2299	< 2200
Fem. 15–16	2100+	1900– 2100	1700– 1899	1500– 1699	< 1500
Male 17–20	3000+	2700– 3000	2500– 2699	2300– 2499	< 2300
Fem. 17–20	2300+	2100– 2300	1800– 2099	1500– 1799	< 1500

The test supplies tables calibrated by age group and has separate ones for younger and older athletes. All distances given in the tables here are in metres.

The columns giving average (**Ave**), below average (**Ave-**) and **Poor** allow everyone to learn whether or not their heart and lungs are in good condition, without resorting to expensive testing facilities.

Figure 10 12-minute run test tables (older athletes)

Age	Exc	Ave+	Ave	Ave-	Poor
Male 20-29	2800+	2400– 2799	2200– 2399	1600– 2199	< 1600
Fem. 20-29	2700+	2200– 2700	1800– 2199	1500– 1799	< 1500
Male 30-39	2700+	2300– 2700	1900– 2299	1500– 1999	< 1500
Fem. 30-39	2500+	2000– 2500	1700– 1999	1400– 1699	< 1400
Male 40-49	2500+	2100– 2500	1700– 2099	1400– 1699	< 1400
Fem. 40-49	2300+	1900– 2300	1500– 1899	1200– 1499	< 1200
Male 50-59	2400+	2000– 2400	1600– 1999	1300– 1599	< 1300
Fem. 50-59	2200+	1700– 2200	1400– 1699	1100– 1399	< 1100

The test also provides approximate VO_2 max scores, a small number of which are given below:

Figure 11 12-minute run test: approx. VO_2 scores

Distance covered (in metres)	VO_2 max (mls/kg/min)
3000	55.7813
2800	51.3100
2600	46.8388
2400	42.3675
2200	37.8962
2000	33.4249
1800	28.9537
1600	24.4824
1400	20.0111
1200	15.5395

Sprint tests

Sprint tests are a measure of speed (see page 76). They can be used in several ways either to monitor performance or as part of a specific or general programme of training. They can also be used to measure velocity, acceleration and maximum speed, and to see whether someone has an aptitude for a particular sport or activity.

Sprint tests are not only useful for sprinters but for games players who need speed over a short distance. A tennis player does not need to be fast over 100 metres but speed around the court is a considerable asset, just as it is for the scrum half in making a break to set up an attack. The most common sprint tests are:

- 30-metre acceleration test: monitors athlete's ability to build up acceleration from a standing (or block) start
- 60-metre sprint test: measures sustained speed over a longer period
- 30-metre flying sprint test: usually performed as part of a longer sprint and a time is taken for a specific 30-metre 'flying' section of it
- the Running-based Anaerobic Sprint Test (RAST test): perhaps the most sophisticated test as it measures both power output and fatigue levels.

There are similar (water-based) tests for swimmers and an ergometer test for cyclists.

The 30-metre acceleration test can also be used to predict time over the longer distances of 60 metres, 100 metres and 200 metres. This can be useful in a variety of sporting activities. *Predicted* times can be compared to *actual* times and this is also useful when the period of training does not include running full time-trials over 100 or 200 metres.

The sit and reach test is a test for flexibility

Figure 12 30-metre acceleration test: predicted results

	Predicted times				Predicted times		
30	60	100	200	30	60	100	200
3.5	6.38	9.93	19.38	4.7	7.88	12.28	24.80
3.6	6.52	10.13	20.25	4.8	8.01	12.47	25.20
3.7	6.64	10.32	20.68	4.9	8.13	12.66	25.60
3.8	6.77	10.53	21.10	5.0	8.25	12.85	25.99
3.9	6.89	10.73	21.52	5.1	8.37	13.04	26.38
4.0	7.02	10.93	21.94	5.2	8.49	13.23	26.78
4.1	7.14	11.12	22.35	5.3	8.61	13.41	27.16
4.2	7.27	11.32	22.77	5.5	8.85	13.78	27.94
4.3	7.40	11.51	23.17	5.7	9.10	14.15	28.70
4.4	7.52	11.70	23.58	5.9	9.33	14.51	29.46
4.5	7.64	11.90	23.99	6.0	9.45	14.70	29.83
4.6	7.77	12.09	24.40	–	–	–	–

The sprint test has the advantage that it can be run in a sports hall, so training and monitoring can be done when the weather outside is poor.

Sit and reach test

The sit and reach test is a test of flexibility (see page 00), and is used particularly in connection with the hips, hamstrings and muscles of the lower back.

The legs must be fully extended and the soles of the feet flat against the bench or box being used for the test. Measurement is taken at the point reached by the fingertips past the line of the toes. It is essential that a lengthy warm up is done before this test in order to avoid injury to the muscles of the lower back or the hamstrings. Performers are normally allowed two attempts, with the best result being the one recorded. Figure 13 shows guidelines for a 16 year-old performer.

As with other tests, this won't increase flexibility itself. There needs to be a progressive programme of flexibility work in between the tests for any progress to happen.

Although the sit and reach test is useful as a basic flexibility test for potential gymnasts, remember that flexibility is important for participants in all activities, whether or not it is identified as a specific component of fitness.

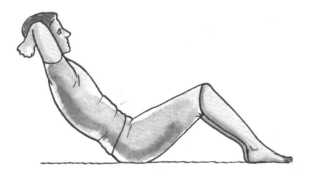

Figure 13 Sit and reach test tables

Gender	Exc	Ave+	Ave	Ave-	Poor
Male	28cm+	24–28cm	20–23cm	17–19cm	< 17cm
Female	35cm+	32–35cm	30–31cm	25–29cm	< 25cm

Note: These figures are for 16 year-old performers

Press-up/sit-up test

Press-ups and sit-ups are used as a test of muscular endurance (see page 75) in:

- the arms and shoulders (press-ups)
- the abdominal region (sit-ups).

Both of these activities can be modified for safety reasons. It can be dangerous for individuals with above average bodyweight to attempt full press-ups, using the knees as pivot points reduces this risk. Sit-ups should never be performed with straight legs because of the risk of abdominal or internal injury.

Press-ups and sit-ups can be used as part of specific or general exercise programmes (with safety precautions observed) and can also be used to monitor and evaluate progress in terms of general well-being or preparation for a specific activity.

Figure 14 Guidelines for 16 year-olds (sit-ups)

	Exc	Ave+	Ave	Ave-	Poor
Male	> 26	25-26	23-24	21-22	< 22
Female	> 23	21-23	19-20	17-18	< 17

Figure 15 Guidelines for adults (sit-ups)

	Exc	Ave+	Ave	Ave-	Poor
Male	> 60	54-59	46-53	39-45	< 38
Female	> 50	44-49	37-43	31-36	< 30

Agility run test

This test, also known as the Illinois Agility Run, is an excellent test to discover the kind of agility and balance (see page 80) that is required of potential team and racquet games players.

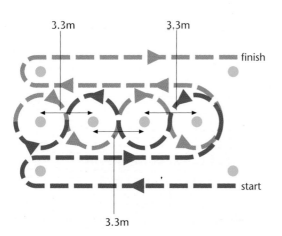

A course for an agility run test

The stork stand test is a test for balance

The test requires the performer to complete the course as fast as possible with times being converted into a score. The performer must avoid the cones by weaving in and out of them or the test is invalidated. The recorded score is usually the fastest of two permitted attempts. Detailed scoring tables are provided with the test (see Figure 16).

Figure 16 Agility run test scores

Gender	Exc	Ave+	Ave	Ave-	Poor
Male	15.9 secs+	15.9–16.7 secs	16.8–17.6 secs	17.7–18.8 secs	< 18.8 secs
Female	17.5 secs+	17.5–18.6 secs	18.7–22.4 secs	22.5–23.4 secs	< 23.4 secs

Note: These times are for 16 year-old performers.

Stork stand test

The stork stand test measures balance (see page 80). It is sometimes also referred to as the 'blind stork test' during which the subject is required to undergo the test whilst blindfolded.

The person stands on both feet with hands on hips and lifts either leg and places the toes of that leg against the knee of the supporting leg.

Timing begins when the person is steady and continues until 'wobbling' becomes difficult to control. The procedure is then repeated with the position of the legs reversed.

Tasks

1. As a group, perform the seven tests.
2. In small groups, produce 'rank order' lists for the whole group for each test, and identify any individuals whose test results suggest that they have a particular ability.
3. Identify any sports that you think someone with such results would be good at.

Fitness training principles

Planning and monitoring a personal exercise programme

In preparing your six-week personal exercise programme, you will need to bear the following in mind:

- **the individual and their requirements**
- **specific fitness component(s)**
- **warm up and cool down.**

The individual and their requirements

First you must establish the purpose of the programme. There are many reasons why an individual may wish to undertake a personal exercise programme: to lose weight; to feel good about themselves; to regain fitness for competition after a lay-off because of injury, and so on. Whatever the reason may be, it is an important factor, as it will influence the nature and possibly the severity of the programme you plan.

The individual is also important. Whether they are male or female, young or old or have previous exercise experience must all be considered so that any exercise programme can be safe, purposeful and appropriate to their needs. Any initial assessment may also need to be reviewed every so often in the light of progress and any change in circumstances: for example, illness or periods when commitments at work make it difficult to find time to exercise.

If you are planning a programme for someone else, you need to check that they have medical clearance before starting any programme of exercise, for whatever purpose.

There are two important questions to be asked when planning a personal exercise programme:

- Is the programme for general health and well-being?
- Is the programme for a specific activity?

The answer will affect the type of programme you plan.

Specific fitness components

In assessing the needs of the individual, it will become clear whether a general programme of exercise is required for health and well-being or whether the programme is intended as preparation for a specific activity.

With regard to the content of the programme, a general exercise programme will need to address a wide range of fitness components. An activity-specific programme will need, in addition, to concentrate on those components identified as relevant.

In designing a general fitness programme, you might decide to work on all the components of fitness but to select no more than four or five of them to be part of any one exercise session.

In order to vary each session, it might be appropriate to include some pure fitness components and some skill-related ones. If the programme were based on three 30-minute sessions per week, some components would then be worked on once and others twice.

This imbalance could quite easily be addressed. During the second week of the programme the sessions could be modified so that the reverse applied. This would produce a balanced programme over a two-week cycle of sessions, as shown in these two charts:

Week 1

Fitness component	Week 1	Week 2	Week 3
Cardiovascular endurance	✓		✓
Muscular endurance		✓	
Strength	✓		✓
Flexibility		✓	
Agility	✓		✓
Balance		✓	
Co-ordination	✓		✓
Speed of reaction		✓	
Timing			✓

Week 2

Fitness component	Week 1	Week 2	Week 3
Cardiovascular endurance		✓	
Muscular endurance	✓		✓
Strength		✓	
Flexibility	✓		✓
Agility		✓	
Balance	✓		✓
Co-ordination		✓	
Speed of reaction	✓		✓
Timing		✓	

Whether you keep the programme like this or vary it would depend on how the performer progressed. If you identify weaknesses in some components of fitness, for example, in cardiovascular endurance and co-ordination, these aspects might require some additional sessions, replacing others – possibly as a temporary measure.

It is also possible that while the programme is underway the performer might identify a particular activity that they would like to pursue. If a suitable level of general fitness has already been reached, it might be necessary to re-design the programme from scratch, so that this new purpose can be accommodated.

Specific activity

Your personal exercise programme might be designed to improve fitness for a specific activity. Nevertheless, it might still be advisable to ensure that an all-round programme of exercise came before more specialised work unless this was clearly not necessary.

However specialised an activity, all the components of fitness should be addressed at some point.

In the case of a shot-putter, for example, flexibility, agility and cardiovascular endurance might be addressed as part of both warm up and cool down routines so that the body of the training programme can concentrate on the event-specific components. In contrast to the general exercise programme, this specific programme might include:

Programme designed for a shot-putter

Fitness component	Week 1	Week 2	Week 3
Cardiovascular endurance			
Muscular endurance		✓	
Strength	✓		✓
Flexibility			
Agility			
Balance			
Co-ordination	✓		✓
Speed of reaction		✓	
Timing	✓		✓

This specialisation is reflected in the fact that there are fewer components as part of the programme, with only two or three being addressed in any single session. This allows for more time to be spent on each one as a measure of its importance in the activity concerned.

In reality, the contents of the programme will vary according to the time of year and whether training is concentrating upon building power and strength, or on developing technique and speed.

Warm up and cool down

The warm up

The body needs to be well prepared for physical exercise. It is not such a good idea to suddenly begin strenuous activity and expect the body's systems to adapt instantly and without injury.

As part of this preparation for physical exercise, we need to ensure that certain basic requirements are satisfied:

- the pulse rate should be gradually raised to a level approaching that experienced during the activity

- joint flexibility should be addressed through a series of moderate (but not violent) stretching and mobility exercises
- the skills or movements that are part of the activity should be part of the warm-up process
- the performer should become mentally focused on the activity to come.

Where possible the warm-up environment should resemble that of competition. So, for example, cyclists should warm up on an ergometer or rollers, swimmers should warm up in a practice pool, weightlifters should warm up in a weight-room, etc.

The warm-up environment should resemble the environment of the event

All training should start with a warm up and end with a cool down

The cool down
The purpose of the cool down is, in many respects, the exact opposite of the warm up. The body has been working at maximum level in competition or in training and must be allowed to return gradually to its normal resting state.

Just as it is not advisable to begin activity suddenly and without preparation, it is also inadvisable to stop just as suddenly.

During exercise, the heart rate is much faster during exercise than normal and blood is being pumped around the body at a higher rate. Suddenly stopping this physical activity will cause blood to pool in the body's tissues, which effectively then has nowhere to go.

If the heart slows down too quickly, this can also slow down lactic acid removal from the

muscle tissues and cause muscle soreness when the body finally cools down.

By continuing to exercise gently we continue to promote blood flow and allow the body's systems to return to their normal everyday level of working without harmful after-effects.

Tasks

1. Explain why it is important for the needs of the individual to be taken into account before any programme of exercise is embarked upon.
2. Which components of fitness would you emphasise in the exercise programme for
   a a games player
   b an artistic or rhythmic gymnast?
3. Explain why it is important that any warm-up activity includes elements of the sport in which the performer is about to take part.

The application of training principles

In developing a training or exercise programme it is essential to be aware of the principles that govern the way in which the body responds to physical exercise.

These training principles include:

- overload
- specificity
- progression
- peaking
- reversibility.

Overload

Quite simply, we can only achieve improvements in most aspects of physical performance by forcing the body to work beyond its current known limits. In other words, we overload it.

This applies to improvements in strength, in endurance or in physical mobility, all of which can only be achieved by working at or beyond the present limits of performance. In order to make improvements, therefore, the workload must be progressively increased during training.

The body responds by adapting itself to this increasing workload, providing the increase is achievable. This process is known as adaptation and represents the period when the body learns to accommodate the new demands being made upon it.

Overload must be *progressive* (normally within five or ten per cent of existing capability) but not *excessive*.

The rate at which the body adapts to new and higher demands will vary depending on the nature of the work and the experience of the performer. A beginner will make much more

rapid advances than someone who has already made considerable progress. Adaptation will also vary from one component of fitness to another.

As adaptation occurs and the body becomes relatively comfortable working at a higher level, targets should be re-assessed and loads increased to enable further progress to be made. (See FITT principles at the end of this section, page 112.)

Progressive overload can be achieved by increasing:

- the resistance (e.g. adding 5kg to the weight being lifted)
- the number of repetitions (the number of times an exercise is done in one set)
- the number of sets (e.g. 1x10; 2x10 etc.)
- the frequency of sessions (how many per week)
- the intensity of sessions (how much work per session)

It can also be acheived by reducing the rest periods within each session.

Specificity

The simple principle to be applied here is that for training to be most effective it must be specific to the activity for which it is intended.

This does not mean, for example, that a cyclist cannot benefit from any training that does not involve riding a bike, but it does mean that any work done *off* the bike must have the improvement of performance *on* it as its main purpose.

A hammer-thrower will only spend a certain amount of training time actually throwing the implement: much of their winter training will be spent developing explosive strength and the speed, agility, balance and co-ordination required to control a heavy implement while it is in motion.

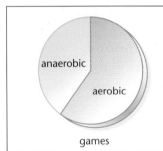
games

weightlifting

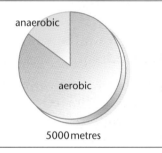
5000 metres

Specificity and energy system use

Specificity training must also take into account that different sports use different energy systems. Training sessions must develop the energy system – aerobic or anaerobic – that is appropriate for the activity.

A 5000 metre runner, for example, relies heavily on the aerobic energy system and training will consist almost entirely of activity designed to increase aerobic capacity. However, there will also be times – either in the middle of a race or as it draws to close – when flat-out bursts of speed require a switch to anaerobic energy; so that element must be built into the training programme as well.

A games player will utilise both anaerobic and aerobic energy. In a game of football, netball or hockey, players will spend some of their time during the game running at a medium pace or even walking (aerobic exercise). However, they will also quite regularly need to sprint for a pass or to keep up with an opponent (anaerobic exercise).

In complete contrast to the 5000 metre runner and the games player, the weightlifter will spend only a few seconds in executing their performance. All the (anaerobic) energy is directed into one massive effort, which may have to be repeated perhaps fewer than half a dozen times during a whole competition, with recovery periods following each performance.

This is entirely anaerobic and apart from some general fitness and flexibility work, should represent a major part of the training programme.

Progression

Whether a programme of exercise is intended to promote general health, is being undertaken just for fun, or is in preparation for a specific activity, improvement in one or more areas of performance would normally be part of its intended aims.

For this to occur, there must be **progression** built into the programme. That is, the nature and range of the training activities should be such that they are geared towards moving from general aims to specific targets or objectives within a specified time frame.

It is also important that once the performer has advanced beyond the novice stage, these targets or objectives should be ones that are agreeable to both the performer and the teacher or coach.

Progression can be achieved by ensuring that three specific pathways are followed:

- **easy to difficult**
- **general to specific**
- **quality to quantity.**

These three concepts embrace the training principles of overload, adaptability, specificity and peaking (see opposite).

Figure 17 Progression in exercise and training

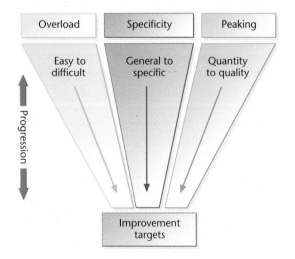

By gradually increasing the training load (*overload*), progression is achieved over a period of time (*adaptability*). At the same time the precise nature of the activities within the training programme should change from being general fitness activities to those that are more closely event-related (*specificity*). A swimmer, for example, would progress from a general weight-training programme to one containing movements which simulate the actions involved in their particular stroke.

At a time agreed by the athlete and the coach, training activity should also begin to reduce in quantity and increase in quality in order to be approaching competitive level as the season or major competition draws nearer (*peaking*).

The importance of progression in any training programme will of course depend on the needs of the individual or group and the requirements of their particular activity. Does a young tennis player simply want to be good enough to play socially, or are there higher targets in mind?

Just how good do you want to be?

The emphasis on progression in the training programme of an international athlete should be self-evident but for someone who simply wishes to exercise for good health it may not be so important. Someone who exercises purely for fun or to stay reasonably active may be happy to reach a certain level of fitness and simply maintain it. In such a case, the coach or instructor must bear this in mind and vary the activities from time to time in order to avoid sessions becoming monotonous and boring.

Peaking for a major competition is vital for many performers

Peaking

Professional athletes (and their coaches) know that they can only operate at their absolute best for a limited period of time. It is vitally important that peak performance coincides with a major event or competition.

Part of the purpose of building progression into a training programme is to ensure that certain performance targets are met. **Peaking** is all about ensuring that these targets are achieved at the right time.

- **Progression produces performance**
- **Peaking produces performance at the right time.**

Peaking is not a totally predictable science – we sometimes read of an Olympic favourite who loses out in the final only to break a world record in the days following the 'big one'. Clearly, peaking at the right time, in the right place, is the aim of most top sportsmen and women, but only a few seem to get it right all the time.

For those athletes for whom peaking has a major significance, each phase of training will be timed so that final preparations coincide with a selected major competition.

This phasing or breaking down of training into sections is also referred to as periodisation of training. The objectives of each phase for a track athlete might be as follows:

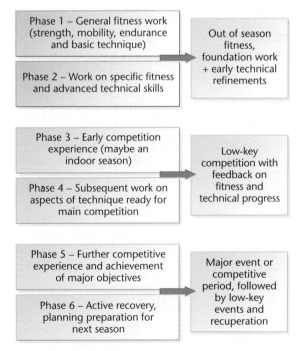

Periodisation of training

Peaking for a specific event is more common in some sports than it is in others. Some athletes may prepare for a handful of events a year. Others must produce the goods on a weekly or even twice-weekly basis in league competition.

Reversibility

The process of **reversibility** applies to most aspects of physical performance. It means that the effects (or improvements) of training will be lost at about one third of the rate at which they were gained. This means that if you stop doing an activity, perhaps due to an injury, then fitness is lost at the rate of one-third of the time it took to gain.

A beginner who makes remarkable progress in the space of just a few weeks and is then injured may lose all that has been gained if inactivity lasts for more than a couple of weeks or so. A performer who has spent many years developing fitness will therefore lose rather less than the novice in the same period of time.

The effects of training are easier to maintain if they are gained over a longer period of time and are lost more slowly when training ceases.

This is very important for those sportsmen and women who must develop several components of fitness for their event. If specialisation requires them to stop work on (for example) strength, in order to develop technique, then careful account must be taken of the effect that this might have on their performance.

If strength levels deteriorate too far, then any advantage gained by improving skill levels may well be counter-productive. In this situation many performers would prefer to reduce the level of strength training rather than cut it out completely.

Similarly, mobility must always be part of training or exercise routines. This allows the improved range of movement developed in early training to be maintained during other phases of training.

FITT principle

We have now looked at the principles that govern both the acquisition of fitness and the rate at which it is lost when training (or a part of training) is discontinued. We have identified the various components of fitness and how, although they are all important, some activities demand particular attention to some rather than others. We have also noted that in some instances, where general health and enjoyment might be the aim, it is better to address all the fitness components equally without any undue concentration on one or another.

There is a set of principles (or guidelines) to help us ensure that all the aspects of training referred to so far are included in any programme of exercise. They are usually referred to by the acronym, **FITT**.

FITT principles suggest that all training or exercise programmes – whatever their purpose should include the following:

- **Frequency** of training or exercise
- **Intensity** of training or exercise
- **Time** of training or exercise
- **Type** of training or exercise.

Frequency
The number of training sessions per week, or per fortnight, will vary according to individual need. At a basic level, experts suggest that three sessions per week is the minimum frequency that is needed to acquire and maintain healthy fitness levels.

In the case of aspiring or established top-level performers this might be considered inadequate. It is not uncommon for some top-level performers to train two, or even three times *per day*.

Intensity

The intensity of the training (how hard we work) is also governed by the purpose of the programme. Someone who is sufficiently motivated to take up an exercise programme for the sake of their health would not want to be confronted with a programme that was so difficult that it put them off training altogether. But for aspiring gold medallists the work in training must be at least as hard – if not harder – than they will find in competition.

For general improvement of health it is essential that the heart rate is raised to between 60 and 85 per cent of the maximum heart rate (MHR) for a specific age group. This is known as the safe training zone. The MHR is calculated by subtracting your age from 220. A person who is 30 years old would therefore have an MHR of 190. Calculations then allow us to work out the training zone for effective training:

> **The lower threshold for training is 60% of MHR:**
>
> $$\frac{190 \times 60}{100} = 114 \text{ beats per minute}$$
>
> **The upper threshold for training is 85% of MHR:**
>
> $$\frac{190 \times 85}{100} = 162 \text{ beats per minute}$$
>
> **The safe training zone would be between 114 and 162 bpm**

Some athletes are known to exceed these limits by considerable margins and those involved in extreme endurance events may have an MHR in excess of 220 bpm. For the rest of us, though, training in the upper limits of such zones should certainly only be done if approved by a doctor.

Time

For most people, around 30 minutes or so of brisk activity is sufficient to raise the heart rate above the 60 per cent of the MHR threshold. At the other end of the spectrum, international athletes frequently train for up to two or three hours per session. Most of the time between sessions has to be spent recovering and relaxing.

Type

The type of training activity will reflect the specific needs of the individual or group concerned. Some groups are activity focused, such as the local badminton class that also serves as a general fitness activity. Others will include an all-round programme of exercise designed for fun and variety but which also happens to serve the needs of those requiring a basic level of fitness.

For those with a more serious intent the nature of the training activity must reflect the needs of the sport. The training programme must graduate from general fitness work to highly specialised activity relating to a particular sport. In team games, much time might be spent in developing tactical approaches and set pieces, whereas a gymnast may spend hours just working on a better dismount from one piece of apparatus.

Generally, as adaptation/improvement occurs, a review of FITT will be needed.

Tasks

1 Explain how you would apply the principle of overload to an exercise programme for general fitness.
2 Explain the difference between overload and progression.
3 How would an improvement in performance or personal best time influence the application of FITT principles to an athlete's training programme?

Training methods

Training for specific activities

There are a number of training methods that can be used either in general exercise programmes or in preparation for specific activities. All of them can be adapted for use in a wide range of training and exercise programmes.

The most common methods of training currently in use are:

- **circuit training**
- **continuous training**
- **fartlek training**
- **flexibility training**
- **interval training**
- **weight training.**

Circuit training

Circuit training is based upon the completion of a series (or circuit) of exercises. It is probably one of the most flexible forms of training and circuits can be devised to develop any of the components of fitness (see pages 74–83).

Circuits are most commonly set up indoors but can just as easily be outdoors where conditions will permit this. For many years military recruits have endured circuit training in the form of an assault course.

A circuit normally consists of between six and ten exercises or workstations, each of which is intended to exercise a particular group of muscles or fitness component.

Each exercise is completed in turn until all have been done. A short rest is taken before completing the circuit again.

It is usual to complete between three and five circuits in one session but only where the instructor is satisfied that all members of the group are able to do so safely.

There are several alternative procedures for setting the targets (number of repetitions) for each exercise. The most common is to base this on the maximum number of repetitions that can be completed for each exercise in one minute.

Half of each maximum figure then becomes the 'set' number of repetitions to be completed at each station on the circuit. After several sessions, maximums are then re-set – hopefully showing some improvement as a training effect – and the sessions then start again with new, higher 'set' figures for each exercise.

Some advanced performers can complete three circuits with gradually reduced rest periods until they become one continuous circuit.

Select the right training for the right event

At that point the time is recorded for each one and progress is thereafter measured by the improvement in the time taken to complete all three circuits without a break. This form of circuit training is particularly beneficial to games players who need to be on the move all the time and perform a whole range of body movements.

Circuits can be general or specific and they can be designed to develop any of the individual components of fitness.

It is also possible to design skill circuits with activity at each station intended to work on a particular aspect of skill. A skill circuit for soccer players might include:

- dribbling in and out of cones
- heading a ball at a target
- rebound passing against a wall or target
- 'keeping up'
- shuttle-runs, passing a ball at each end
- continuous goalkeeping.

Some of the above would need partner assistance.

Circuits can be designed to increase the volume of work done – for improving fitness; or to concentrate on the speed with which activities can be performed in order to simulate competitive conditions.

Continuous training

Continuous training requires the body's demand for oxygen to be matched by its oxygen intake. If activity levels are too high then the body runs out of oxygen. If they are too low, then training benefit is not obtained. (Look back at intensity of training and safe training zones on page 113.)

Continuous training improves endurance (aerobic capacity). Common examples of continuous training are aerobics classes, cycling, dancing, running and swimming.

Continuous training is very effective for improving all-round fitness. It is also used as part of training by long-distance swimmers, cyclists and ultra-distance runners. All of these need to be able to perform at a steady state for extended periods of time.

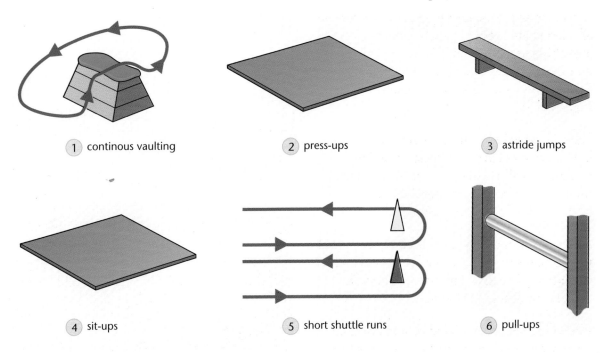

1 continous vaulting   2 press-ups   3 astride jumps

4 sit-ups   5 short shuttle runs   6 pull-ups

A simple, general exercise circuit

Fartlek

Fartlek is a Swedish word meaning 'speed play'. It is another form of continuous training designed to stress the aerobic energy system. Because steady-paced running is interspersed with almost flat-out bursts of speed, it also develops the anaerobic system.

Traditionally, it took place in the forests of Scandinavia and then in the countryside in the UK. It is often now transferred on to an athletics track or the road, where signposts, lamp-posts or other features act as markers for short bursts of sprinting. 'Sprinting for the next lamp post' is a favourite activity amongst racing cyclists when out on training runs.

This form of training has a wide range of sporting applications and these include distance runners who need to be able to change their pace during a race, games players who employ both aerobic and anaerobic energy systems and cyclists who in road races need to be able to sprint suddenly

The principle of fartlek training works on a bike too

in order to make a surprise attack or to respond to one being made by an opponent.

Flexibility training

This form of training is relevant to all sporting activity, although it is often overlooked.

Moving or stretching the tendons surrounding a joint to a point marginally beyond their normal limits is the normal way of developing and maintaining flexibility. This can be done either by the performer or with assistance from a partner. This is normally referred to as:

- **active stretching**
- **passive stretching**.

Active stretching
Active stretching is when the performer can stretch some joints easily without any assistance. The hamstring muscles and their tendons can be stretched without undue difficulty by grasping the ankles or toes while in the sitting position. Some stretches at both the hip and shoulder joints can also be performed unaided without too much difficulty.

Passive stretching
In some cases a full range of movement can only be achieved with assistance from a partner or coach. Lateral extension of the arms behind the plane of the shoulder joints is difficult to achieve unassisted. It is best performed with a partner holding the arms from behind and pulling them gently backwards in order to achieve maximum stretching at the shoulder joint. Here the performer would be passive, allowing the assistant to perform the stretching movement but taking care not to stretch the joint beyond a safe point.

Joints should be stretched to the point just beyond their limit and this position should be held for around ten seconds.

Active stretching of the hamstrings and adductor muscles

These movements should NOT be performed violently and joints should not be extended beyond that of marginal discomfort.

Stretching and/or flexibility exercises form part of:

- **the training programme**
- **a warm-up routine.**

As part of the normal training routine, flexibility exercises should cover all the major joints of the body. This should take place three times per week in order to maintain flexibility at its optimum level.

Flexibility should also be part of any warm-up routine prior to competition and before any training sessions. This should address two aspects:

- **whole body flexibility**
- **attention to event-specific joints.**

For some activities, such as hurdling, javelin throwing and fast bowling, specific joints come under considerable stress and free movement must be maximised before any competitive or training activity. In activities such as dance or gymnastics *all* joints must be mobilised.

Interval training

Interval training is a more clearly defined form of training, with specified periods of activity followed by short rest periods. Progression is achieved by moderating the periods of work (repetitions) and the periods of rest. Repetitions are normally completed in sets and the number of sets can also be modified according to the stage of training.

This method is very popular with performers whose events cover a precise distance. Each period of activity is followed by a short rest period (interval) and both the activity and the rest can be varied according to the activity and the level of fitness.

Swimmers, track cyclists and athletes all make heavy use of interval training, which allows them to work at under- or over-distances and set precise targets in terms of times.

A distance can be broken down into smaller units (e.g. 4 x 200m or 8 x 100m = 800m), each of which can be completed at a pace that would not be sustainable for the whole distance.

By slowly reducing the interval (rest) periods and adjusting the periods of work, it is possible for an 800-metre runner, for example, to gradually progress from 8 × 100m to 4 × 200 metres and then to 2 × 400 metres – all run at race pace or faster.

Time trials over the full race distance take place periodically so progress (or lack of it) can be monitored. Time trials are particularly useful in the period leading up to a major competition, allowing both athlete and coach to assess realistically likely performance.

In order to build up endurance, repetitions will often total more than the race distance so that an 800-metre runne might perform 6 × 200m repetitions rather than just 4 × 200m. Once target times have been achieved, they can be adjusted so that the whole process starts again.

Longer periods of work are used to develop endurance whilst shorter periods are used to develop speed and hasten the process of lactic acid removal.

> **Interval training for an 800-metre runner**
> Personal best = 2 min.
> Target time = 1 min. 50 sec.
>
> **Phase 1:**
> Schedule
> 6 x 200m in 29 sec. : 3 min. rest
> 6 x 200m in 29 sec. : 2 min. rest
> 6 x 200m in 29 sec. : 1 min. rest
> 3 x 400m in 58 sec. : 3 min. rest
> 3 x 400m in 58 sec. : 2 min. rest
> 3 x 400m in 58 sec. : 1 min. rest
>
> NB: This process may take many weeks to complete.
>
> Time trial 800m = 1 min. 56 sec.
>
> **Phase 2 (re-set time and intervals):**
> Schedule
> 6 x 200m in 27 sec. : 3 min. rest, etc.
> 3 x 400m in 27 sec. : 3 min. rest, etc.
>
> NB: Rests (intervals) are between each run. Where more than one set is performed, longer rest would be required between each set. For example, two sets of 6 x 200m with 3 min. rest would be one training session. Once achieved, sessions would consist of two sets of 6 x 200m with 2 min. rest, etc.

Tasks

1. How might the principles of circuit training be adapted to meet the needs of
   a rugby team
   b a group of throwers?
2. Explain why continuous training would not be a major component in the training of a weight-lifter.
3. How might interval training be of specific help to middle-distance runners and swimmers?

Weight training (isometric and isotonic)

Like circuit training, weight training is a very adaptable method of improving several aspects of fitness, although it is perhaps most widely used as a means of developing muscular strength and/or endurance. Traditionally, all exercises were performed using free weights, usually in the form of either dumb bells or barbells, but modern weight training machines of the multi-gym or individual station type are now more widely available and far safer than free weights.

Weight training makes use of the principle of progression by gradually increasing the amount of weight handled in a range of exercises, each of which is intended to develop a specific group of muscles. These are often referred to as progressive resistance exercises.

In a similar manner to the principles behind interval training, the amount of weight, the number of repetitions performed and the periods of recovery between sets of repetitions can be used to adjust the workload to suit the needs of the individual and the activity for which the training programme is intended.

As with other forms of training, weight training can be used as part of a general programme of exercise. This has become very popular with the arrival of a large range of training devices which make the activity both appealing and relatively safe. Even so, it is strongly advised that such activity should not be undertaken without expert advice and it should only take place in schools under qualified supervision.

For the serious sportsperson, weight training is probably the most common and effective means of developing both muscular strength and endurance. This is largely because exercises can now be devised that will use specific muscle groups in a way that almost exactly replicates their action during competition. It also means that the principle of specificity is built into many training programmes.

Muscular strength
When using weights to develop muscular strength, all work should be at, or near maximum capability in the exercise being performed, and the number of repetitions performed in each set should be low (usually six or less).

Once the maximum weight that can be handled for each exercise has been established, the weights used should be at least 85 per cent of that figure. A routine for a thrower with a maximum squat of 200kg wishing to develop upper leg strength might therefore be:

> 3 sets of 6 repetitions, each set performed with 170kg on the leg press machine

This might be alternated with pyramid sets as follows:

> 1 set of 5 repetitions with 170kg
> 1 set of 3 repetitions with 185kg
> 1 set of 1 repetition with 200kg (max)

Using a leg press machine: far safer than free weights – especially with heavy loads

As in circuit training, maximums are occasionally re-tested and the schedule adjusted accordingly.

Muscular endurance

To develop muscular endurance the number of repetitions needs to be much higher than when exercising for muscular strength. This requires between 20 and 30 repetitions of each exercise to be performed at around 50–60 per cent of maximum capability. Pyramid sets would not be used as there would be no endurance benefit gained from performing one repetition, regardless of the weight.

A triple-jumper who might need both muscular strength and endurance could usefully adopt both strategies beginning with:

3 sets of 30 repetitions with 100kg on the squat machine, leading to:

3 sets of 30 repetitions with 120kg, then:

work on strength as the competitive season approaches

In both cases there would be three sessions per week in the close season and this might be reduced to one session during the competitive period to ensure that earlier strength and/or endurance gains are not lost.

Weight training, including work with light, free weights, can also be used as part of flexibility training. In many cases a small weight can help to obtain a full range of movement at a particular joint without necessitating the use of a partner. However, care should be taken in both the choice of the weight used and the manner in which the exercises are performed.

One of the criticisms of weight training as a means of developing all-round fitness is that it does not involve sufficient whole-body activity to improve aerobic endurance. It is therefore important to ensure that some aerobic work, such as running, cycling or swimming should be included in all fitness programmes – even where aerobic endurance is not a major requirement.

It is possible to introduce some free weight exercises into circuit training, and if they are mixed with some aerobic activities such as shuttle runs, step-ups or astride jumps, this can provide a good way of combining the development of both muscular *and* aerobic endurance needed by many games players.

Isometric and isotonic contractions

Muscles produce movement by contracting (see page 12). There are two main ways in which muscles do this – **isometric** contractions and **isotonic** contractions. Isometric contractions are for stabilising movements. The muscle holds part of the body still (or tries to). In this case, the muscle tenses, but it doesn't lengthen or contract. In isotonic contractions, the muscle moves: either lengthening or contracting. Pull-ups are a good example of this: the biceps contract isotonically to pull us up, then lengthen isotonically to lower the body down again.

Most forms of muscle training use isotonic contractions: we move the muscles we are training. But there is also a form of training using isometric contraction. Basically, this involves pushing against an immovable force, so that the tension of isometric contraction is produced. The harder you push, the harder you ask your muscles to contract isometrically, until you reach your point of maximal isometric contraction.

Training using this principle is known to produce considerable strength gains – within very specific limits. It can be done in the weights room by using weights well beyond the performer's capability. This provides a resistance against which maximum force can be exerted but no movement is involved.

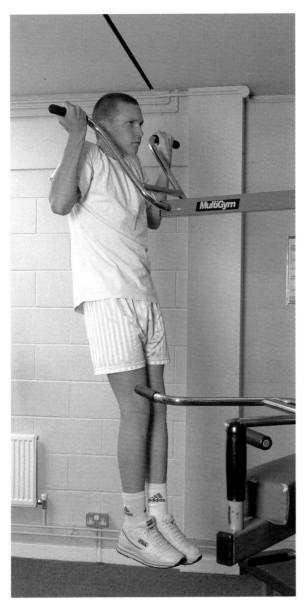

Pull-ups use isotonic contractions

Pushing against a scrummage machine: isometric training

This method of developing strength was at one time very popular but this is no longer the case. Maximal isometric contraction trains muscles to contract at a greater speed than can be produced by isotonic contraction of muscles, which is why this method produces a big gain in strength. But this strength gain only applies to a very small range of movement. This is because muscle fibres are being trained to contract only at one particular point rather than through a full movement range.

Tasks

1. How can flexibility be incorporated into a programme of weight training?
2. Explain the difference between isotonic and isometric exercise. Use examples to illustrate your answer.
3. Why would a weight training programme designed to develop muscular endurance involve more repetitions than one intended purely for strength improvement?

Training effects

Immediate short-term effects of exercise

There are a number of physiological changes that take place in the body following the start of exercise. Many of these processes will have begun during the warm up and will be further accelerated during the high levels of activity in a competition. For your course, you need to know about these short-term effects of exercise:

- breathing
- pulse rate
- circulation
- muscles
- sweating.

Breathing

As exercise starts, the rate of breathing rises quickly as the nervous system warns the body that exercise has begun. This will occur initially during warm up and again at the start of 'exercise proper'. In some cases the nervous system may kick in even before activity has commenced – a sort of early warning system.

As the rate of breathing rises, more air is drawn into the lungs and the muscles involved in the act of breathing begin to work harder so that breaths become much deeper. The increased volume of air delivers more oxygen to the bloodstream in response to the demands of the working muscles.

Pulse rate

In response to this increased respiration level, the nervous system triggers a faster heart rate so that a greater volume of blood can be pumped around the body. The stroke volume

remains constant but the increased heart rate delivers oxygen to the muscles at more than double its resting rate.

The pulse and respiration rates will continue to rise until the volume of oxygen required by the working muscles is met. The pulse rate will then level off as the body reaches a 'steady state' of activity. In the case of purely anaerobic exercise (e.g. 100 metres), these rates may continue to rise even after activity has ceased.

Circulation

The circulation of blood increases as the level of activity rises in order to meet the increased demand of the muscles for oxygen. Although the major blood vessels dilate (become larger) to allow this to happen, there is a corresponding narrowing of those blood vessels not directly involved in the activity: for example, those that supply the digestive system. This makes sure as much blood as possible gets to where it is most needed.

The onset of exercise: how does the body respond?

Muscles

Blood vessels in the active muscles dilate in order to accommodate the increased blood flow generated by exercise. The blood temperature also rises, which is important, as this produces more efficient muscle action. A rise in blood temperature from 37° to 41° produces a 15 per cent increase in muscle performance.

This increase in temperature is also of benefit to the connective tissue at the points where the working muscles are attached to bone (muscle tendons). It increases their blood supply and greatly reduces the likelihood of tears, strains and muscle pulls during the early part of a performance. Much of this process will already have begun during the warm-up period.

Figure 18 Improvement in sprinting performance with rise in muscle temperature

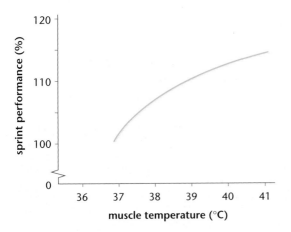

Sweating

Sweat is produced as a response to the normal build-up of body heat. This process is accelerated during increased levels of physical activity. Sweat is released through the sweat glands through the pores of the skin and is a means by which some waste products are removed from the body. It is also part of the process by which the body is cooled. Sweat contributes to a cooling of the surface of the skin and a constriction of the small blood vessels near its surface.

Long-term effects of exercise

General well-being

The more general long-term effects of exercise include a fitter, healthier body. This is often accompanied by an improved sense of well-being – we feel better able to cope with the demands of life generally. Our bones become stronger due to a higher level of calcium production and our tendons and muscles become more elastic due to repetitive stretching through an increase range of movement. Usually, exercise produces a better, healthier appetite and improved sleep patterns. There are also benefits to be gained in terms of our general lifestyle. As fitness improves, we might expect to feel better about life in general and far more capable of coping with the stresses and strains of everyday living.

General well-being is usually improved by exercise, providing that the level of activity undertaken is reasonable to begin with and progresses at a rate which is sensible. Over-training can cause injuries, tiredness and tissue damage, which in the long-term is counter-productive.

As well as promoting general well-being, you also need to know about other more specific long-term effects of exercise:

- **effects on the heart**
  - **heart rate**
  - **stroke volume**
  - **cardiac output**
- **circulatory system**
- **breathing**
- **body composition**
- **muscles**
- **rate of recovery.**

Effects on the heart

The long-term effects of training and exercise on the heart include the enlargement of the heart chambers and a thickening and strengthening of its muscular walls.

This means that the heart itself beats much more strongly and delivers blood to the circulation system far more efficiently.

Heart rate

The resting heart rate is much lower in trained athletes than in others. This enables the heart to do the same amount of work as before but with much less effort. Its capacity to work at higher levels and for much longer periods is also increased.

Stroke volume

As a result of regular training, the stroke volume (that is, the amount of blood pumped from the heart in one beat) can, in some cases, increase to more than double that of an untrained person.

Cardiac output

The increased efficiency of the heart produced by regular training means that the total amount of blood it can process in one minute is much increased. This is the result of the combined effect of a larger stroke volume and a lower resting heart rate.

Circulatory system

Arteries become larger and more elastic as a result of regular training, and this reduces blood pressure. There is also more haemoglobin in our blood because we are producing more red blood cells.

There are much lower levels of fat in the blood because our body has picked up its ability to use fat as fuel. Regular training also means we have a greater capacity to process lactic acid during exercise.

Breathing

Regular exercise has the long-term effect of increasing the number of alveoli in the lungs and this, in turn, has the effect of enlarging lung capacity. This allows a greater volume of air (containing oxygen) to pass through the lungs and into the bloodstream.

This means that we are able to maintain higher levels of activity for a much longer period of time. More oxygen being passed into the bloodstream means we can keep up the supply of oxygen to the muscles for a longer period. There is an improvement in the capacity for anaerobic work because there is a greater amount of energy stored in the muscles before exercise begins.

The increased efficiency of the respiratory system means that the process of gaseous exchange is considerably improved, so that greater levels of carbon dioxide and other waste products can be removed from the body both during and after exercise. Generally, breathing become much easier and we are less likely to get out of breath when performing normal daily tasks that involve a moderate amount of physical activity.

Body composition

Our body composition is affected by regular exercise and training in several ways. Although we are probably not aware of it, our bones become stronger as a result of increased levels of calcium production. Assuming that exercise includes a reasonable level of mobility work, our muscles and their tendons become stronger and far more elastic.

If long-term activity includes a modest amount of aerobic exercise then our body learns to utilise fat more efficiently as a fuel energy source instead of carbohydrate. This means that fat deposits are reduced and this can lead to a reduction in bodyweight.

Muscles

Muscles respond to increased activity over a long period in several ways. Initially they respond by becoming larger (hypertrophy) until they are big enough to cope easily with the work they are being asked to do. This growth in muscle size depends on the type of training and competitive activity.

If very heavy weights are lifted (either in competition or in training), muscle size will increase by large amounts (adaptability) until the muscles become large enough and strong enough for this new level of work to be accomplished.

If medium or light weights are lifted (usually with far more repetitions), muscle size will increase only sufficiently to allow the exercise or activity to be performed comfortably. Any further improvements will be in the area of muscular endurance.

Fast-twitch muscle fibres also increase in size, particularly when either training or competitive activity contain some element of speed or movement.

It should also be noted that periods of inactivity due to illness or injury will result in a decrease in muscle size. This is known as muscle **atrophy**.

Another long-term effect of exercise is that larger amounts of oxygen will be stored in muscle cells. This is particularly beneficial to those involved in anaerobic activity (see page 30). Muscle tendons and the ligaments surrounding joints also become stronger and more flexible.

Rate of recovery

If we undertake a long-term programme of training or exercise, the body adapts so that it is able to cope with these new demands. Eventually, what initially might be very hard work becomes easier and our bodies recover

Regular exercise makes us feel good

from it far more quickly than at the outset of the training programme.

Even when the level of activity is increased (progression), our bodies will eventually learn to cope with this new level. As this happens, recovery will again be faster than before.

Tasks

1 List *three* short-term and *three* long-term effects of exercise.
2 What tests would you use to measure the long-term effects of training on the heart?
3 Using what you know about the long-term effects of training, design a poster to encourage people in your community to join your local gym.

Potential hazards

As a performer, you have a responsibility to be aware of the potential hazards, both to yourself and to others, that may be associated with any activities in which you participate. You should also be aware that the environment in which you work might be a source of potential danger.

For this course, you need to know about potential hazards in the following areas:

- **court areas**
- **the gymnasium**
- **outdoor adventurous activities**
- **the playing field**
- **the sports hall**
- **the swimming pool.**

Court areas

These areas are often used for netball and tennis, but they may also be used for other activities such as basketball and small-sided games of soccer. As well as for games, they

What are the potential hazards of court areas?

are often used for the teaching of skills, some aspects of fitness work and may also be part of the general playground provision of the school. A growing number of schools now also have astroturf areas. These are often used for community as well as school activities.

Litter is often a major potential hazard. Paper and plastic can cause people to slip, even when the conditions underfoot are not wet. Drink cans and other sharp objects can be very dangerous. The school population isn't always to blame for litter on courts if these areas are also open to the local community in the evenings and at weekends.

It is vital to get into the habit of looking over an area to identify and, if possible, remove potential hazards before an activity starts. They might include:

- broken/protruding bits of surround fencing
- nails or splinters sticking out of fence posts
- corners of buildings that are too close to court areas
- wobbly portable posts (e.g. netball), or portable posts with feet sticking out onto the playing area
- surfaces affected by rain, snow, frost or inadequate maintenance
- projecting post-sockets which may not be in use but which may be in the middle of another playing area (e.g. tennis-post sockets)
- nearby windows not protected by grills or fencing.

For your exam, you will need to be able to identify and explain how these and similar circumstances can contribute to possible injury and how this may be avoided.

The gymnasium

The gym has the potential to be one of the most hazardous activity areas. The fact that many gyms are also used as indoor games areas (a purpose for which many of them were never intended) is often a source of problems

Wall bars, window ladders and beam uprights often project into the working floor space, even when they are correctly stowed away. Inadequate or poorly designed gymnasium storage space often means that benches and other portable items cannot be stored easily. All of these objects can be dangerous when an over-zealous game of five-a-side soccer or basketball results in someone being knocked into one of them.

Not in the gym!

Some students never really understand why their PE teacher 'has a thing' about footwear in the gym. Many of today's hard-soled leisure shoes are not suitable for use in the gym. Those with soles treaded like tractor tyres will carry dirt and grit from outside onto a gym floor which make it both unusable and dangerous. This is why shoes worn outside the gym shouldn't be worn inside it.

Before a lesson in the gym, check:

- if the floor is clean, dry and free from dust, dirt and grit
- if items of portable apparatus that aren't to be used have been safely stowed away in the appropriate place
- if items of fixed apparatus such as beams, wall bars, window ladders and ropes have been secured in their 'home' position
- if there are any projections, wall-fixings, hooks or other fittings that have recently become unsafe that you can bring to the attention of your teacher and others in your group
- that fixing bolts or catches are securely in place on equipment to be used (following your teacher's instructions) and that the equipment is safe to use.

In addition to these points, ask yourself whether or not you and others in your group are behaving in a way that is both appropriate and unlikely to cause injury, either to yourself or anyone else.

There are other issues about the use, carrying and storage of equipment that will be dealt with later in this section (see page 137).

Equipment in the gym should be properly stowed away to leave an unobstructed area

Tasks

1 As a group, create your own list of items to check before the start of a lesson on an outdoor court area.
2 Design a poster for your school gym to convince people that they should change their shoes before using the gym.
3 School gyms are often used at evenings or the weekends by people from the local community. Create a list of the potential hazards in the gym for their information.

Outdoor adventurous activities

There are a considerable number of outdoor and adventurous activities, each of which may present its own potential hazards. The key issues applying to most of these activities are that:

- such activities are often set in remote surroundings well away from the school campus
- the environments in which these activities take place are often new to many students and are sometimes harsh, exposed and potentially dangerous.

Adventurous activities take place:

- on land
- on water
- on both land and water!

Activities on land

On land it is likely that the location may be remote. It may be exposed to bad weather and the terrain may be difficult to walk on. These all tell us that the way we behave, the way we are dressed and the way we communicate with each other become far more important than is the case in our normal everyday lives.

Land-based activities include:

- assault courses and other 'challenge' activities
- camping and/or expeditions
- caving and potholing
- cycling/mountain biking
- horse riding/pony trekking
- mountain walking and/or climbing
- orienteering
- rock climbing and abseiling
- skating
- skiing.

Activities on water

If activities are taking place in, or on water then likely hazards may centre upon whether the water is enclosed (e.g. a swimming pool or a small boating lake) or whether it is open or coastal, how deep it is and whether there are dangerous currents. If the activity is also situated in a remote area, then exposure and how close shelter is may also become important.

Water-based activities include:

- angling
- canoeing and kayaking
- rafting
- rowing
- dingy sailing
- windsurfing
- sub-aqua
- surfing
- swimming
- water skiing.

Keeping safe

Each activity carries with it a number of potential hazards. There are specific safety procedures and precautions for each one, which your teacher or instructor will make sure you know about before you can start.

Saying if you are worried or unsure about something is a very responsible thing to do. Your PE teacher or course leader should know if you can't swim or are not very good at swimming before you start an activity on or near water.

Although it may be embarrassing to admit that you have a fear of heights or exposed situations, it is far better to ensure that your teachers know of this beforehand – otherwise you might put yourself and others in danger.

There are some basic potential hazards that apply generally to outdoor adventurous activities. You should *always* bear these in mind:

> **If you're up high you can fall off!**
> **If you're on water you can fall in!**
> **If you're in water you can sink!**

So in terms of your own sensible precautions you need to ensure that:

> **You don't fall off!**
> **You don't fall in!**
> **You don't sink!**

For example, any activity involving climbing, whether this is on a local climbing wall or elsewhere, will involve working at height and will carry with it fairly obvious hazards. If the weather is poor or footholds are in poor condition, such hazards will be accentuated. In mountain biking, the nature of the terrain will mean that far more concentration will be required simply to stay in the saddle than would be the case on urban or suburban roads.

Some potential hazards in this situation are pretty clear

If you visit the same centre or repeat the same activity several times, then it will be easier for you to foresee hazards than if you are trying an activity or a venue for the first time.

The playing field

Playing fields, like court areas, can be difficult to close off effectively. These open spaces are often used for all kinds of activities by ordinary members of the public. Sometimes such use is officially approved but often it is not. The fact that playing field areas are also sometimes used for general recreation by the whole school during good weather can add to these problems.

Potential hazards include dog faeces, broken glass, crushed drink cans and general litter. These are far more noticeable on tarmac and other hard areas than they are on grass playing areas. The grass on rugby pitches is often quite long and this can hide potentially dangerous objects unless it is closely inspected. As with hard court areas it is important to get into the habit of checking for hazardous objects before using a playing field.

Other potential hazards that may cause injury include:

- long grass, uneven or pitted surfaces
- frost, ice, snow or heavy rainfall
- use of sticks or poles as goal or boundary markers where someone could fall onto them
- wobbly portable goalposts – that could fall onto someone
- rugby goalposts without protective padding at their base
- corner flags or other marker posts that aren't flexible and which could snap
- people wearing smooth-soled footwear, particularly in contact sports: this can be very dangerous.

Students like yourself have little or no control over the use of such equipment or the maintenance of playing field areas. But as a responsible student, you should develop an awareness of these potential hazards and bring any apparent problem to the attention of your teacher(s).

For the exam, you will need to be able to identify and explain how these and similar hazardous circumstances can arise; how they may contribute to possible injury and how, as students, you might assist in the minimisation of potential hazards.

Rules reduce risk!

All activities, including those that normally take place on the playing field have their own specific guidelines regarding safety. These can normally be found in publications produced by the national governing bodies of the activities and should be studied closely as part of this GCSE course – particularly in respect of those activities you intend to do for your practical assessment.

These guidelines cover personal and playing equipment as well as appropriate behaviour. All of these factors can contribute significantly to the reduction of any likely dangers that may be inherent in the activities themselves, as well as the places where they are performed.

Tasks

1 List the reasonable precautions that students could take in terms of their own behaviour while on a day visit to an outdoor pursuits centre.
2 What are the specific hazards that need constant vigilance in relation to your own school playing fields?
3 Give your view on the extent to which you think it is appropriate that students take some degree of responsibility for monitoring the environment in which they work.

The sports hall

In many respects a sports hall is simply a larger version of a gymnasium and this is particularly so when considering likely sources of potential hazards. The floor is an important area to be aware of and, as in a gymnasium, students can contribute most positively by adopting a sensible attitude to their own behaviour, by wearing appropriate footwear and by becoming aware of likely sources of danger.

Because sports halls are larger than gymnasia, they are often intended to accommodate more than one activity at the same time. Students must therefore be mindful of other activities going on as well as their own.

Where ball games or activities involving other 'projectiles' are concerned, remember that more space often means a greater velocity and therefore added risk of injury!

Sports halls often have more than one means of access and the number of students entering or leaving during activities may be greater than in a gymnasium.

Multi-activities can easily multiply hazards

Coming into the sports hall itself can be potentially hazardous, as you are entering an area where balls may be flying around. Entrance doors to sports halls usually have glass or perspex panels in them so you can check that it is safe to go in. Doors separating other areas from the main sports hall should be designed to be self-closing. You should report any doors that aren't closing by themselves to your teacher.

Golf, cricket and tennis are all examples of outdoor activities that can also be played or practised in a sports hall. In the case of the first two of these, although it is normal for activity to take place within a netted area, specific guidelines as to behaviour and conduct must be strictly followed. Both of these can be hazardous activities, particularly if participants fail to accept that they have a responsibility to behave appropriately.

As in the gym, potential hazards in the sports hall are:

- apparatus and other equipment which is not in use must be safely stored or fastened away in order to minimise obstacles
- walls and other surfaces should be smooth and free from projections or jagged/sharp objects.

In some cases, a sports hall complex may also include facilities such as a weight training or fitness room, a projectile room or a climbing wall. There are specific hazards associated with each of these facilities and uses and guidelines should be clearly displayed and strictly followed. If this is not the case then this should be brought to the immediate attention of a member of staff.

The swimming pool

Whether you use a pool in your own school or a nearby municipal facility, you need to know about potential hazards in terms of:

- **pool-based activities**
- **the pool and its immediate surroundings.**

Pool-based activities

The governing bodies of activities that take place in water such as the ASA and the RLSS, publish clear guidelines on all aspects of safety and potential hazards. You should study these as part of this GCSE course – particularly if you intend to do pool-based activities for your practical assessment.

The biggest potential hazard in any swimming pool is the people who use it. As students of physical education your priority should be to ensure that your own behaviour and attitude are not called into question.

The pool and its immediate environment

People can drown in swimming pools. This potential hazard is behind most of the regulations and restrictions on behaviour in the pool and its immediate surroundings.

Your teacher or instructor will greatly appreciate any co-operation in what is potentially a high-risk activity. To ensure safety it is essential that you:

- do not enter the water until you are told and in the way that you are told
- engage only in activity you are asked to perform
- leave the water when and in the manner you are instructed.

In all swimming pool areas, health and safety regulations require that definitive 'Do's' and 'Don'ts' are clearly displayed. As a general guide, potential hazards might include:

- wet floor surfaces around the pool and in showering and changing areas – a danger of slipping

What are the potential hazards of swimming pools?

- diving boards, spring boards and other poolside apparatus – diving should not happen where people are also swimming
- the use of flippers, masks (other than swimming goggles) or any other swimming aids in water by inexperienced swimmers
- venturing out of your depth if you are a poor or novice swimmer
- submerged grating or grilles – there is a danger of swimmers being caught on these and held under water.

Above all you should remember that your teacher or instructor has a collective responsibility for a whole group of students. It is therefore totally unreasonable to expect them to be responsible for the irresponsible.

Remember that you may be asked to describe or explain the nature of hazards in connection with any activity you intend to offer for practical assessment.

More activities, more hazards

Swimming pools are sometimes used for other activities such as the teaching of basic canoeing skills or for training and testing in life-saving and personal survival.

Each of these activities presents its own hazards. Although your teachers are responsible for ensuring that you are made aware of them, it is your co-operation in avoiding such hazards that is the key to safe practices being effectively carried out.

Personal survival activities should not involve weak or novice swimmers. It is therefore very important that your teacher or instructor is aware of any poor swimmers in your group. Your teacher may be well aware of your capabilities and will have passed this information on to any other instructor. However, it is advisable to check that this is the case.

In the case of personal survival activities, particularly those requiring the wearing of everyday clothing, your teacher may like to arrange the group in the water so that the stronger swimmers are close by those who are less experienced. This is sometimes referred to as the 'buddy system'.

As a general rule, swimmers and canoes do not mix. In other words, unless it is required as part of a capsize drill or rescue drill, swimmers should not be in the water when canoeing or other activities are taking place. An exception here might be where swimmers are placed in the water to assist students with drills, but these should be advanced swimmers and/or experienced canoeists.

In all types of pool-based activity, a sensible and responsible attitude by all participants greatly reduces the risks involved.

Tasks

1. Design a notice to be displayed on the entrance to a sports hall that is most used by students. Include in it a list of *six* important safety issues.
2. Put yourself in the place of your teacher. What specific information would you need to obtain and what instructions would you give to a group of students before their first swimming session in a local authority pool?
3. Explain why basic canoe training in a pool is less hazardous than in open water.

Rules and safety regulations

You should make sure that you know what the rules and safety regulations are for your four chosen games or activities so that you always play safely and do not risk injuring yourself or others. It will also help you to get good marks for your coursework.

This information will also be very useful in the exam on questions about risk assessment and potential hazards in activity areas. You can bring into your answers what you know about the safety regulations in your chosen activities.

The rules of a game or activity are frequently related to safety. They are often designed to minimise the potential hazards of a sport, and to stop inappropriate behaviour, which is a very common cause of injury in sport and physical activity. These rules and conventions can apply to behaviour both on the playing area and off it.

Knowing the rules helps prevent accidents

133

Prevention of injury

Minimising risk

There are risks associated with virtually every physical activity or sport as well as with the surroundings in which they take place. Recognising and removing potential hazards is very important for helping to prevent injury.

There are also other factors that must be taken into account by organisers, teachers, coaches and performers. Your course identifies the following as areas that should be given particular attention:

- **appropriate level of competition**
- **clothing/footwear**
- **correct technique**
- **knowledge of appropriate safety procedures**
- **lifting/carrying/placing equipment**
- **personal protective equipment**
- **rules, codes, laws**
- **warm up/cool down.**

Listen to advice: injuries can be avoided!

Appropriate level of competition

The most important element in any assessment of risk is the people involved. One factor in the prevention of injury is ensuring that performers compete at an appropriate level. Problems can be associated in some sports with big differences between contestants in:

- **age**
- **sex**
- **physical size/weight.**

Age
In many sports there are now regulations controlling the age of participants playing together in competition. Normally this is limited to playing in your own age group, although in some circumstances better performers are allowed to play in an age group that is one year higher. An under-15 soccer player might therefore play against under-16s, but not against older competitors. Just as importantly, competitors are often not allowed to play in a younger age group.

The reasons for this are to do with safety – older contestants will tend to be bigger and stronger – and also with ensuring a good match. We develop advanced skills, rather than being born with them. Young players are therefore more likely to get something out of their sport if they play against people of their own age, rather than constantly being outplayed by much older players!

Sex
Although many girls mature physically much earlier than boys, there is a point at which boys become generally bigger and stronger than girls. Some mixed sports will then constitute an unnecessary risk, especially if

Tag rugby can be played as a mixed game because it reduces contact

the boys have not yet developed control over their strength.

It is important to identify both the activities and the age at which segregation is desirable for the sake of safety. In sports where this is an issue (such as in soccer), governing bodies publish regulations on such matters. The English Schools Football Association, for example, do not support the playing of soccer by mixed groups beyond the age of eleven years purely for reasons of safety. In rugby, where heavy physical contact is an essential feature of the game, mixed activity is strongly discouraged. The recent growth in popularity of 'tag rugby', however, means that a form of the game can be played without undue risk of injury to smaller and lighter participants.

Size
Being big is an advantage in some games and activities (a rugby forward, for example), but it can be a disadvantage where mobility and speed are crucial. There is a safety concern when people of very different sizes play together for the same reason as with some mixed games. Where physical contact is high, a larger person can do more accidental damage to a smaller person – if they fall on them, tackle them incorrectly, block them inappropriately, etc.

It is only relatively recently that the big differences in size that can exist between students of the same age group has become a cause for concern in connection with potential injuries. As yet there appear to be few official restrictions in the UK to prevent students of widely differing size and weight from competing in the same competition in high contact sports.

New Zealand, home of the famous All-Blacks, has for many years operated an age/weight group system in its schools and junior rugby. In the UK, teachers can take some effective measures during normal lesson activity to ensure that obvious mismatches do not occur.

Ironically, boxing, a sport which finds little support in schools today, is one of the few that enforces weight classifications within the same age group.

Tasks

1. Make a list of those sports in which you think mixed participation should not be encouraged. Give reasons why you think this should be so.
2. Discuss in your group the advantages and disadvantages that might result if rugby and other contact sports were played in weight/size categories instead of in age groups.
3. If physical education is designed to prepare students for life as adults, why should we limit participation in most sports to specific age groups? Give your view.

Correct clothing and footwear

In most sports, clothing fulfils three major purposes:

- **identity (e.g. team strips)**
- **protection from cold weather in the warm-up period (e.g. a tracksuit)**
- **suitability/safety for the specific activity.**

Additional clothing, like a tracksuit, is usually removed once full activity is under way, unless it is clothing kept on for religious purposes, like a turban, for example. In some circumstances, play on redgras or astroturf surfaces might justify the wearing of tracksuit bottoms or long sleeves in order to minimise the risk of skin burns or grazing.

Fashion trends should not play any part in determining what is the correct clothing for physical and sporting activity. Sports clothing is designed to be appropriate for the activity in which it is to be worn and to minimise injury. Most schools rightly have a policy on what clothing is suitable, and what is not.

Footwear
In all spheres of practical activity the use of unsuitable or ill-fitting footwear can be dangerous.

Wearing shoes that are not correctly laced up may be trendy, but it can also cause a broken or sprained ankle – or a black eye to whoever happens to be in the line of fire when it parts company with its wearer. Tight-fitting footwear can easily cause blisters as well as long-term damage to the feet.

For many sports, you need studded or spiked footwear in order to allow you to get purchase against the ground and avoid slipping over. These should be fixed tightly in place and studs particularly should be checked for rough edges that could cause a dangerous gash in someone else's thigh.

Jewellery
Rings, earrings, necklaces and other items of personal adornment can cause injuries. They are prohibited in most physical contact sports. If such items must be worn for religious reasons or simply cannot be removed, they should be taped and covered in such a way that they cannot cause injury to the wearer or to others. An earring ripped out of an ear lobe during a rugby game, for example, can leave a wound that requires stitching and possibly a lasting and disfiguring scar.

Correct technique

The most obvious benefit of using the correct technique is that of improved performance. However, it is also important to realise that in many sports the correct technique is also the safest. You should consider this aspect of performance in terms of your own safety as well as that of others.

Personal injury
A mistimed or poorly executed tackle in rugby can result in serious injury to the tackler, just as poor technique in a gymnastic vault or pole vault can also cause injury to the performer.

There are also risks to others: a poorly directed discus, javelin or hammer can result in serious injury to anyone who happens to be in its flight path or near to where it lands. A badly hit or undercut hockey ball can have equally disastrous results.

Good technique is therefore not only important in producing good performances but it can often significantly reduce the risk of injury to yourself and to others.

Knowledge of appropriate safety procedures

Safety procedures are the means by which activities are conducted safely and, as far as is possible, any risk of accident or injury is removed. All the things we have been looking at in this section can count as safety procedures. You will need to know about the safety procedures that are particularly relevant to your chosen activities to do well in this course – and to enjoy your coursework!

Safety procedures are important in:

- setting up/preparing for an activity
- ensuring safe play
- completion and clearing away.

It is vitally important that javelins are transported correctly

Lifting/carrying/placing equipment

An amazing number of students seem to believe that the equipment they use will magically transport itself to its appointed place when it is needed and just as magically, put itself away again afterwards! Another common misapprehension is that the teacher will easily manage this task while they also supervise changing rooms and prepare for their next lesson.

The key words here are *co-operation* and *safety*. It is important for everyone who uses equipment to help ensure that it is returned, properly and safely to where it is stored.

In some cases, it is impossible for equipment or apparatus to be moved safely without the assistance of others. Sometimes, there is a danger of serious injury if this is not done in a very precise manner – javelins, for example.

Your teachers will have given clear instructions on lifting, transporting, fixing, securing and storing gym apparatus. You should be aware of the following in respect of *any* physical activity in which you are likely to be involved:

- how to take out and move or carry equipment safely
- how to make secure and use equipment safely
- how to put away equipment safely.

Tasks

1. Identify the key safety procedures in your four chosen activities.
2. Explain why it is important to know how to lift and carry equipment in the correct manner.
3. Give *two* examples from *one* of your chosen sports that illustrate how you can minimise risk of injury to yourself and to others.

Personal protective equipment

Performers in some sports wear protective equipment to minimise risk. In some school sports, it is compulsory to wear personal protection, such as helmets for batsmen and wicket keepers in school cricket and shin pads in all competitive soccer games – including school matches.

In sports such as rugby, where there might appear to be a clear case for the wearing of personal protection, it is left to the discretion of the individual. There are mixed views on this topic. Some authorities argue that the wearing of shoulder pads and mouth guards should be compulsory, while others say that the feeling of being protected encourages players to be more reckless than they normally would in what is already a very physical game.

Rules, codes, laws

The rules of any sport aim to:

- establish a framework of rules, which as far as possible ensures fair competition
- set clear guidelines as to what is safe and fair practice and to identify a range of sanctions for use against offenders.

There is sometimes a great temptation for performers to adopt a 'win-at-all-costs' attitude, especially when there are so many examples of blatant and dangerous foul play in the wider world of sport. There is, however, no justification for breaches of rules or codes of conduct. Not obeying the rules may cause serious injury to yourself or to other performers.

Many sports involve heavy physical contact or the use of potentially dangerous implements. Every player has a responsibility to control their own behaviour irrespective of the nature of the activity or the provocation of others, both on and off the field of play.

In your own case, it is essential that you are familiar with the rules of activities in which you take part, *including* any references to unsafe and dangerous conduct. This is particularly relevant in those activities you intend to offer for practical assessment/external moderation.

Warm up/cool down

A poorly or hastily executed warm-up routine (see page 106) can easily result in a pulled muscle, a strained ligament or long-term damage to a joint capsule. A proper warm up is not only important as a preparation for good performance but is also a crucial element in the avoidance of injury,

A proper warm up reduces the risk of injury

particularly in the first few moments of activity.

Similarly, a gradual and controlled cool down (see page 107) also contributes to the most effective recovery from physical exertion. This helps to promote a return to normal body function and reduces the likelihood of stiffness and soreness in the post-competitive period. Bearing in mind that today's athletes train almost every day, a properly conducted cool down can contribute greatly to lessening the risk of injury at the beginning of the next period of activity.

Remember that the OCR specification requires you to be able to, '*describe and explain, using a variety of examples, various ways to minimise risks...*', in any of the areas covered in this section of the text. You can use relevant knowledge from other parts of the course, and from your coursework, to good effect here.

Good personal hygiene

This topic may at first seem out of place in a section of the text dealing with risk assessment in physical activity. However, although personal hygiene (or rather lack of attention to it) may not directly contribute to injury in sport it can certainly cause uncomfortable and sometimes incapacitating ailments.

Amongst the most common infections that affect active people are **athlete's foot** and **verrucae**.

Athlete's foot

Athlete's foot is a fungal infection that is normally spread in swimming baths, saunas and shower areas. The main area affected is between the toes and on the soles of the feet. There is often redness, soreness and sometimes severe blistering associated with this infection. Various cures, usually in powder form, are available from a pharmacy but severe infection may require medical attention.

Verrucae

Verrucae are a form of wart, sometimes also referred to as plantar warts. They are caused by a virus and differ from ordinary warts only because they become embedded into the feet as a result of the pressure caused by walking. Although various forms of self-treatment creams exist it is advisable to take medical advice first.

In both the above cases, the risk of infection can be greatly minimised by carefully drying your feet after showering or bathing. Wet or damp feet that are then put into socks or tights and footwear provide an ideal environment for the growth of viruses and fungal infection.

A simple personal hygiene regime will help to considerably reduce the risk of a whole range of minor infections, including uncomfortable skin rashes and viral and fungal infections:

- shower, using soap, after all physical activity
- dry off thoroughly before dressing
- always change your clothes after physical activity – this includes underwear
- make sure personal items of PE/sports clothing are washed after each use.

Tasks

1 What are the rules and regulations on the personal protective equipment for your chosen activities?
2 Choose *one* of your own sports and give an example of how the referee or official can help minimize the risk of injury to players.
3 Why might having athlete's foot or a verruca affect your ability to participate in a sport or physical activity?

Injury treatment

Signs and symptoms

These terms are often confused, so do be clear as to what each one means:

> - **Signs: what you can see for yourself – swelling, bleeding, bruising, pallor of the skin, etc.**
> - **Symptoms: what the injured person can tell you – pain, discomfort, nausea, etc.**

Treatment of simple performance injuries

If injuries do happen, it is your teacher or coach's responsibility to help the injured person. Any injury is serious or potentially serious, and requires professional treatment. *Never attempt to treat an injured person yourself*, even if you know how, unless your teacher permits this.

For this course, you need to know what the signs and symptoms are of simple performance injuries – the sort of injuries that happen quite often in sport and physical activity. For the exam, you may be asked to explain how they happen and describe how they should be treated. You are certainly not expected to be expertly informed or capable of treating, potentially serious or life-threatening injuries.

For this course, you need to know about:

• blisters	• ligament injuries
• concussion	• muscle injuries
• cuts/grazes	• tendon injuries
• dehydration	• winding
• exhaustion	• RICE.

Blisters

Blisters form when the skin repeatedly rubs against another surface and causes friction. A tear occurs between the upper layers of the skin and, although the outer surface of the skin remains unbroken, fluid seeps into the space immediately beneath it. The most common site for blisters is on the feet but the hands can also be affected, particularly if you are participating in an activity such as rowing of canoeing for the first time.

Never deliberately burst or pop a blister, as this might cause infection. If the skin remains unbroken, protective padding or cotton wool together with a short break from activity will normally take care of the problem. Larger blisters may need to be drained and this should really be done under medical supervision. If the skin is broken then the blister must be disinfected and covered in order to prevent infection.

Injuries should only be treated by professionals

Concussion

Remember that all knocks to the head are potentially dangerous.

Concussion is normally the result of a severe blow to the head, which causes jarring of the brain against the inside of the skull, and swelling of the brain's surface. In cases of suspected concussion, there are various signs to look for – the subject may be unconscious, although this is usually temporary; they may be pale and be breathing in short little breaths; they may be cold and have a fast pulse. If conscious, they may appear to be drowsy (sleepy) and unstable, and may be confused about where they are and what they were just doing.

In all cases of suspected head injury, it must be brought to the immediate attention of a member of staff or other person in charge. Medical attention must be sought as a matter of urgency. Until medical help arrives, make the injured person as comfortable and warm as possible. Try to ensure (gently) that they remain conscious and do not offer water or other drinks – even if they ask for it.

Cuts and grazes

In most physical activities, whether competitive or otherwise, cuts and grazes are a fairly regular occurrence.

A graze is when the top layer of skin is scraped off, often as a result of falling and sliding across a surface. The signs are a red, raw patch on the skin, and the symptoms are pain felt at the grazed area. Cuts are when the skin is cut open and blood is lost – the sign of a cut is bleeding and the symptoms, again, are pain from the cut area.

Most grazes and cuts are not serious and can be covered with an antiseptic dressing after making sure that the wound is clean. They will then normally heal quite quickly and with very little inconvenience.

Deep cuts can be very serious because they can cause a lot of blood loss. Blood is vital to the body (see page 28). There is also the additional risk that a muscle or tendon may also be damaged, or even an internal organ. In these circumstances, treatment must be administered by qualified medical personnel. Your teacher will press down on a clean dressing over the wound or squeeze the sides of a wound together to reduce blood loss until help arrives. If the wound is on an arm or leg, this should be raised in the air to reduce the amount of blood flowing to it.

Dehydration

Dehydration (see page 85) most often occurs in sport as a result of excessive perspiration combined with an inadequate fluid intake – conditions often found in fairly long endurance events. The loss of body fluids at any time can be serious, but it is much more so if it occurs at a time of high energy expenditure, as the body can't cool itself down.

Dehydration and exhaustion often present similar outward signs

The signs of dehydration are similar to those of exhaustion: performers look exhausted and may be unsteady on their feet. The symptoms are a dry and tacky feel in the mouth, dizziness, a feeling of extreme weakness, sickness, and a difficulty in maintaining balance and co-ordinating movement.

Sensible but immediate fluid intake (re-hydration) is the best course of action. If the person doesn't feel better quite quickly, medical help should be sought. Serious dehydration (loss of more than fifteen per cent of body fluid) which remains untreated can cause seizure, brain damage or in some cases death.

Exhaustion

This condition is often associated with activities in extreme environments, which are sometimes also in remote situations.

The subject may be exhibiting one or more of the following signs, which are similar to dehydration (see above):

- extreme difficulty in co-ordinating their movements
- low temperature
- dilated pupils
- weak pulse
- pale, moist skin
- fainting spells.

They may also complain of:

- headaches
- sickness and/or dizziness
- extreme physical weakness.

If exhaustion is related to extreme heat or cold, action should immediately be taken to cool, or warm the subject, as appropriate. If the location is not remote or help can easily be summoned, this should be done immediately.

In remote situations, or when medical assistance is likely to be delayed, a warm (or cool) environment should be maintained by wrapping the subject in blankets or additional clothing to maintain body warmth. Conversely, if the person is over-heated, cool them down by loosening clothing, fanning and applying lukewarm cloths to the forehead – and if possible, areas around the armpit and groin.

Electrolyte drinks can be given (sipped) or slightly salted water. This is to replace the essential electrolytes and fluids lost. Drinks containing either alcohol or caffeine are dangerous as they may interfere with the body's ability to regulate its own temperature.

Injuries to ligaments, tendons and muscles

These injuries normally take the form of:

- **strains**
- **sprains**
- **tears.**

Strains
A strain is an injury to a muscle and/or tendon, which is often caused by overuse, excessive force or over-stretching.

Sprains
A sprain is an injury to a ligament surrounding a joint and is often caused by a wrench or twist. These injuries most often affect the ankle, knee or wrist joints.

In both the above instances, the most effective treatment is that based on a regime of **R**est, **I**ce, **C**ompression and **E**levation (**RICE**), which we will look at opposite.

Tears
A tear, which may be complete or partial, is an injury caused when muscle fibres are torn away from the tendons attaching them to bones. This usually happens when tendons are over-stretched by a violent movement. Tears can also occur in muscles

and ligaments. RICE is the best treatment for minor tears (see below), while major tears often require surgical repair if complete recovery is to take place.

Strains, sprains and tears often happen because performers have not warmed up properly. The signs of injuries to ligaments, tendons and muscles are not obvious as the injuries are internal. In many cases the person will not be able to put weight on the injured part, or will limp if the injured tendon, ligament or muscle is in the leg. The symptoms are pain in the affected area.

Winding

Winding is usually caused by a blow to the abdominal area, which temporarily paralyses the diaphragm. The signs often include great difficulty in breathing or gasping at it, a doubling-over at the waist and the inability to speak. The person should be placed in a reclining, seated position until they regain the ability to breathe.

RICE

The RICE method is recommended for all minor injuries. It should be started as soon as possible and can promote recovery almost from the onset of injury. RICE stands for:

- **Rest**
- **Ice**
- **Compression**
- **Elevation.**

Rest
Rest means stop playing! All injuries will get worse if you to continue to play, and resting gives your body time to recover, to start healing itself and to start fighting any infection.

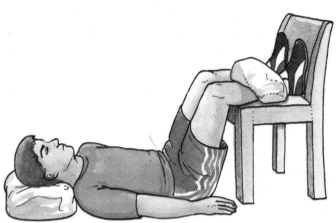

RICE in action

Ice
Ice cools the tissues and constricts the blood vessels resulting in less bleeding or swelling in the affected area. *Do not* apply ice directly to the skin, as it may cause skin burns. Ideally a light, clean cloth should be applied to the affected area so that this may be avoided.

Compression
Using pressure to keep the ice pack on the injury helps stop bleeding and swelling.

Elevation
Elevation means raising the injured part to help reduce swelling and blood loss.

For your course, you need to be able to describe and explain the activities in which the injuries that are described in this section are most likely to be found.

Tasks

For each of the following injuries, describe the signs, symptoms and treatment, and give *two* examples of activities in which these injuries are likely to occur:
a blisters
b muscle, tendon and ligament injuries
c dehydration.

Performance

As manager of a top football team at half time in the FA Cup, what would you be talking about to your team? Unless you were a very unusual kind of manager, you would be talking about their performance in the first half and what they need to do now to win the match.

TV and radio commentators, newspaper journalists, spectators in the stadium and viewers at home would also be talking about both teams' performance: their strengths and their weaknesses – what they have done well, and what they have not done so well. Each player in the match would certainly also be thinking about their own performance and that of their teammates and the opposition. They would be thinking about how to do better in the second half.

Performance is a very important part of your PE GCSE. You will be marked according to your performance in the activities you have selected for your coursework. For one of your activities, you will also carry out an analysis of either your own or another student's performance, which will get you more marks. You will learn a lot in your course about the factors that affect performance and about ways to improve performance through training. You will be expected to show your knowledge of these factors in an exam at the end of your course and to build this knowledge into your practical coursework, which will get you even more marks!

Coursework

In your GCSE PE coursework, you will be assessed by your teacher according to how well you perform in each of your chosen activities under applied conditions. Your performance will be marked according to its strengths and weaknesses in five main areas. These five areas tell us what things your teacher will be looking for in your performance.

First of all, your teacher will assess your performance in terms of how effectively you:

*   select and apply advanced skills and techniques
*   select and apply tactics, strategies and team skills.

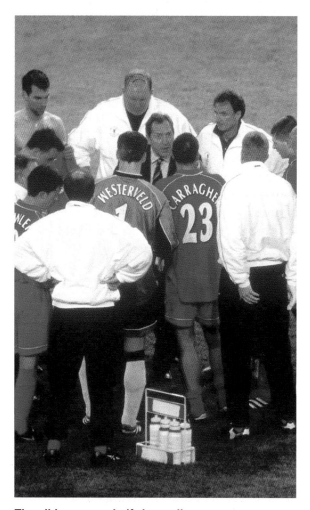

The all important half-time talk

Your teacher will also assess you in how well you:

- evaluate and improve performance
- adopt different roles in the activity or game
- understand and observe the rules and safety regulations of the activity or game.

We will look at all these areas in more detail in this section of the book.

Target setting

So what exactly are the skills and techniques, the strategies and tactics, the roles and rules that you will be marked against? Your teacher will have a copy of the coursework guidance booklet for this GCSE that contains the criteria, or guidelines, for your activities. They may photocopy the criteria for your activities for you. You can use the criteria for your activities to set yourself targets for improving your performance.

For example, Sarah is doing the PE (Games) GCSE and has chosen basketball as one of her four coursework activities. The coursework guidance booklet has a whole list of the skills and knowledge she needs to build up over her GCSE course. It lists the skills and techniques she will need to be able to do, for example, how to stand when shooting, passing or dribbling; how to perform different shots; the skills required for passing and ball control and the correct footwork skills.

The coursework guidance booklet also has information about the tactics, strategies and team skills Sarah will need to be able to perform and know about. All this information, on different ways a team can attack or defend, on different formations of play for different situations etc., is all going to be great for improving her understanding of basketball and the way she plays as part of a team.

Some of these skills and tactics are things that Sarah feels she can already do: she knows, for example, that she has a really good jump shot. But there are other things in the coursework guidance that she is not that confident about, like dribbling with her left hand, for example. There are also other things that she'd never thought about before – like forcing your opponent onto their weak hand, which sound really useful!

Having all this information at the start of the course gives Sarah an idea of what she needs to work on to be a more skilled basketball player, and a better team player. Evaluation of performance – knowing what your strengths and weaknesses are – is a key part of improving your performance. During her course, Sarah will learn all about ways to improve performance, including different ways of training to improve her skills and fitness.

By the end of her course, Sarah knows a great deal about basketball: the skills required for different situations, different tactics and strategies and when to use them, the different roles in the game and all about the rules and safety regulations of basketball. She has worked on her weaker skills and improved them, and refined her stronger skills so she is now a very good basketball player and a valued member of the school team. She knows so much about basketball, in fact, that she is able to analyse the performance of other players, identify their strengths and weaknesses, and work with them to help them improve their performance.

Tasks

1. Make a list of the skills and techniques you feel confident about in your four chosen activities.
2. Now make a list of the skills and techniques that you feel you need to improve.

Advanced skills and techniques

What are 'advanced' skills and techniques? Because you have been learning skills and techniques in PE since you started school, for a GCSE in PE you are now ready to develop your skills to a higher level – and be tested at this higher, advanced level. Examples of advanced skills and techniques for association football would be, for shooting, shooting with the instep, inside and outside of the foot, with swerve, with either foot, and penalty kicks.

All performers, even top-level performers, spend a lot of time working on both basic and advanced skills. Such skills must first of all be learned – often in a simplified form – before they can be developed to an advanced level of proficiency (see pages 32–41 for more information on skills). This is all information you can use to improve your own performance.

In this course, you need to be able to demonstrate advanced skills in your chosen activities. At the end of your practical activity course, your teacher will watch you perform in each of your activities. The teacher will mark you on how well you can demonstrate advanced skills in your performance – using the right skills in the right situations, and performing them well.

Why is it that we know that David Beckham is pretty good at taking free kicks or that Michael Owen is not bad at beating opponents in defence? It's not because we have seen them both train at these skills, but because we have seen them perform them effectively in matches. Likewise, you may well know people who can perform advanced skills with a football in the playground, for example, but just cannot apply these skills in a game situation. Who is a better footballer – someone who can demonstrate excellent ball control in the playground, but not on the pitch, or someone who can't keep the ball up as many times in the playground, but is good at keeping possession in a game? This is why you are tested on your advanced skills under applied conditions: a game or activity situation. We will look at applied conditions in more detail on page 150.

Top performers spend hours practising skills and technique

Advanced tactics, strategies and team skills

Strategies are plans for how to do well in a competition or match. Tactics are the ways that strategies are put into practice. As well as demonstrating advanced skills in your activities, you will also need to know about the tactics, strategies and team skills for your activities, and be able to select and apply the right ones at the right times.

As with advanced skills, because you are now doing a GCSE, you are ready to move to a more advanced level in using tactics, strategies and team skills in your chosen activities.

For most Games activities, advanced tactics, strategies and teams skills centre on positions and roles in defence and attack and how to apply them in the right way and at the right time.

For rugby union, you would learn about principles of attack – like creating and using space, moves from set positions, creating an overlap – and principles of defence – like slowing play down, or denying space to opponents, one to one marking. You would learn about the advantages and disadvantages of different formations in different situations, and applying set plays in attack and defence.

Tactics and strategies in a game like rugby union depend on team skills as well as individual skills. In games activities, team skills are crucial in making the team's overall performance more effective.

The picture at the bottom of the page shows a shortened line out in an England match. The effectiveness of the line out (a team skill) will depend upon the individual skills of a number of players being performed well, for example, those of:

- the thrower
- two lifters/supporters
- the jumper.

The effectiveness of a line out depends on team skills

Deciding to use a short line out is a tactical decision that has the effect of releasing more players from the line out, who are then free to make good use of any possession that may result from it. Team skills are vital in all games – so, for example, a fast break in basketball or a centre pass pattern in netball both depend on a combination of individual and team skills in order to make them effective. However, not all activities are team games. Many events in athletics, for example, can be done as an individual. In such cases, team skills won't be required, but there are still advanced tactics and strategies to be developed and applied and advanced individual skills are important.

So what would be the tactics and strategies for athletics events like the 1500 metres or the high jump? For the 1500 metres you might decide, based on your evaluation of the competition, to try to lead the field from the front, or to start to put pressure on the leading group after 800 metres. In the high jump, you might decide to enter a competition at a particular height.

As with advanced skills, your teacher can tell you what sorts of tactics and strategies are required in your activities. Some activities may not have tactics and strategies, but it will have team skills such as hill walking. You can use this information to work out your own tactics and strategies (and maybe also team skills) for how you are going to do well in your course. There is more information on page 154 on tactics and strategies, which will be useful both for your coursework and for the written exam.

Tasks

When you watch sport on TV, see how many tactics you can identify being used. What strategies do you think the team or performers are trying to put into practice? How well do you think they are doing, and how could they do it better?

Evaluating and improving performance

As well as looking at how well you can apply your advanced skills and your knowledge of tactics and strategies in your chosen activities, you will also be tested on how well you can identify the strengths and weaknesses in your own performance or other people's performance (evaluation), and how you go about improving your performance.

So how do you tell what the strengths and weaknesses of a performance are? The best managers, coaches and sports commentators are people with an enormous amount of knowledge about that sport. They know all about skill and technique, about different tactics and strategies. They can tell if someone is fit or out of condition, whether a performer is motivated or stressed.

The same goes for the performers themselves – they will know if they could have performed better and be able to see the strengths and weaknesses of other members of their team. The best performers in any sport or physical activity are those who can adapt during the activity itself in order to improve their performance and then go away after the competition or event and train to improve their performance still further.

A vitally important part of being able to evaluate and improve performance is having knowledge about your activity. You need to know what skills, technique or tactics should look like when they are performed by an expert performer. This is called the **perfect model**. By comparing a performance with your knowledge of the perfect model you will be able to see what is going wrong, and make suggestions about ways to put it right.

Evaluating performance is a skill that you will learn as you go through your course.

What you can do to improve performance – particularly training to improve skills and fitness – is covered in detail on pages 98–122.

When you are tested on your four activities, you will get marks for evaluation and improvement. The best way to explain this is probably through examples. So for games activities, for example, a teacher would be looking for how well you carry out warm ups and cool downs and practices and sessions that are designed to improve performance. You might be leading the warm up or practice session yourself, using your own ideas on how to improve the team's performance, for example. You would get marks for how well you make or take decisions during a game to improve your own performance or those of others in the team. How well you 'read' a game and act accordingly is also important.

As with skills, tactics and strategies, the coursework guidance booklet tells you what you need to do to get good marks for evaluation and improvement in your chosen activities.

The perfect model: knowing what a skill should look like

There is also a separate assessment for your ability to analyse performance in one of your chosen activities, which counts for 10 per cent of all your marks. We'll look at this part of the course shortly on page 152.

Roles

All games and activities have different roles for people taking part in them. You have the opportunity to take on different roles in your chosen activities, as well as that of a performer or participant. Examples of different roles and their basic responsibilities include:

- **referee/assistant referee** – enforcing rules and regulations
- **captain** – selecting teams and making tactical decisions before and during a game or activity
- **leader** – organising practices to improve play and leading others through practice sessions
- **coach** – assisting in planning training practices, tactics and strategies
- **choreographer** – planning sequences, routines, movements in dance activities
- **official** – helping with the organisation of an activity and officiating.

If you are studying for the full course PE specification, you need to take on one role other than that of performer or participant. If you are doing the full or short course Games specification, you need to follow more than one role, other than that of performer or participant in your activities.

The responsibilities attached to these roles and the skills required would change depending on the type of activity. Also, you can see that adopting a different role gives you all sorts of opportunities to demonstrate your abilities to plan tactics and strategies and, especially, to evaluate and improve performance.

Rules and regulations

For your coursework, you need to know about the rules, laws and safety regulations of your chosen activities. Rules and conventions in sports and activities are very important – they prevent cheating, encourage fair play and help to minimise the risk of injury to players and participants.

You need to know about the rules and regulations of your activities in order to build up your perfect model: tactics are useless if they break the rules of a sport, for example. This is also crucial knowledge for evaluating and improving performance. In order to be able to award marks as a judge of a gymnastics performance, for example, you'd have to know the rules and regulations as well as the perfect model which applies to the particular performance.

Rules and regulations are also very important for taking on different roles in your activities. Both the referee and their assistants officiating a match need to know all the rules of the game to do their jobs. These three officials also need to be familiar with safety regulations concerning kit and equipment such as corner flags and goalposts and nets. Sometimes the referee has to make other decisions about safety – is the surface safe to play on in frosty or wet conditions? And officials who plan and organise events have to be very aware of safety regulations: marathons or triathlons, for example, have a huge number of safety regulations to consider and make provision for.

Tasks

For one of your activities, pick a role (other than performer), like leader, captain or official that you are interested in. Research what the responsibilities of that role involve.

Applied conditions

In order to see how effectively you can perform in your chosen activities, your teacher will, at the end of the practical activity course, get you to demonstrate your abilities in each activity under applied conditions.

As we saw before, the best way of seeing how well people can perform in a sport or activity is to watch them in a match, competition or event. The photo below shows a linesman's view of a situation in soccer. Do you think the player is offside or not?

Applied conditions are like a cut down version of a full game or event. They allow you to be tested under specific conditions that will allow your teacher to see how well you can perform different advanced skills and techniques and how good you are at applying tactics and strategies.

Off-side or not?

Applied conditions can be designed to see how well you can evaluate and improve performance, what you are like at adopting different roles in your activities, as well as how well you know the rules and regulations of the game or activity.

Let's look at some examples. In a games activity like basketball, we might want to look at advanced skills, tactics, strategies and team skills such as your ability to:

- demonstrate in attack that you can control the ball, pass and move into space, keeping possession for your team
- draw defenders in order to create space for you teammates to exploit
- exploit defenders' weaknesses through individual skills like feint and drive or dummy passing, and through team skills like setting up post play
- work as a team for a particular kind of defensive strategy.

Applied conditions would make it easier for the teacher to see how well you can perform these skills by setting up a situation that is designed to test them. In this case, applied conditions might be a half court game with two teams of three, plus a referee. One team would be attacking and one defending and the aim would be for the attacking team to try to make six passes without losing possession, after which they could try to score. After six attempts, the sides would switch over so the three attackers would be in defence and the defending side would start trying to make six passes and then score.

Applied conditions will also be used for activities that aren't team games. For track and field athletics, for example, you might be asked to show how you would warm up and prepare yourself mentally for an event – as though you were about to take part in a major competition.

Then you might be asked to demonstrate the correct technique in each of your chosen

events. If you were a long jumper, you might be asked to demonstrate a long jump from a shorter run up, which would make it easier for your teacher to assess your approach, take off, flight and landing style.

For running events, you might be asked to run shorter distances than usual. In swimming, you could be asked to swim across the width of the pool rather than the length so that you have to make more turns. All these applied conditions make it easier to demonstrate your skills than in a full activity situation.

Applied conditions might also involve you competing against other students in one or two of your chosen events. Your teacher might ask you about ways in which you could improve your technique, or see whether you know how different weather conditions could affect your performance.

Some more examples of applied conditions could include:

- *educational gymnastics* – plan a sequence of movements over and around six different pieces of apparatus
- *canoeing* – launch a canoe from a jetty or beach, paddle forwards and backwards, demonstrate turning using different techniques, demonstrate a bow rescue
- *jogging* – plan a 1000-metre run over a varied course and describe how you are going to run it and what time limits you will set yourself.

Tasks

Design some applied conditions of your own for your chosen activities. Remember that you will need to test advanced skills, tactics, strategies and (if appropriate) team skills, plus knowledge of rules. You could add in the option of students adopting different roles.

Analysis of performance

In order to improve a performance – either your own or someone else's – you need to know what it is that needs improving: the weaknesses of the performance. You also need to know what sort of things could be done to improve those weaknesses through training or practice sessions. If you are analysing someone else's performance, you also need to be able to feed back your observations to them effectively: without making them cross!

So, the process of analysing performance involves identifying:

- performance strengths
- performance weaknesses.

It will also help to identify and produce:

- suggestions on how improvement could be achieved
- long-term and short-term targets for bringing about this improvement.

As part of your coursework, you will carry out an analysis of performance task for one of your activities. This part of the course carries 10 per cent of the total marks, so it is well worth learning how to do it well. However, learning the skills of analysis of performance will be very useful to you more generally, as they will help you improve your own performance in all your activities.

Let's now look at the skills you need to learn in order to carry out a good analysis of performance.

The diagram above shows a model you can use to think about analysis of performance. It starts when you observe a performance. This means you collect as much information about it as you can. When you analyse a performance, you examine all your

Figure 19 Analysis of performance model

information and think about what it shows in terms of *strengths* and *weaknesses*. An action plan is your suggestions on ways you think a performer could go about improving their performance. Feedback is how you communicate your action plan to the performer. The information should help them improve their performance for the next time you observe it again.

Observing a performance

Observation is the key to analysis of performance. For observation to be effective, you need to know what you are looking at, and what you should be looking for.

For example, if you were watching someone playing basketball, you would need to recognise the different kinds of pass, and know what they are called: a chest pass, a one hand pass, an overhead pass, a bounce pass, etc. You should make sure you have a good knowledge of the correct terminology for the activity you have chosen to do your analysis of performance in. This terminology describes the different skills required in the activity.

Knowing what you are looking for is a great help in analysis of performance. There is potentially a huge amount of information to take in from watching someone perform. If you have made a list beforehand of the key aspects of the performance to look out for, then it will make the task a lot easier. What are the most important skills in your activity? For badminton, for example, you might decide that the key aspects to focus your observation on are the specific types of shot:

Badminton analysis checklist
Check how well these skills are performed:
- Overhand clear (forehand)
- Net shots (forehand and backhand)
- Smash (forehand)
- Smash (backhand)
- Drop shot (forehand)
- Drop shot (backhand)
- Drive (forehand)

Breaking down a performance

Sometimes the performance will involve complex skills or routines, and it may not be as easy to identify particular skills or techniques as in the case of the badminton example above.

For example, a gymnastics performance can be technically very demanding, both for the performer *and* for the observer! There may be a lot of different skills being combined. Also, what about carrying out an analysis of performance over the whole course of a rugby or hockey match – there would be a huge amount of information to take in because of the length of time involved.

A good technique for dealing with complex skills, or situations where a lot is going on, is to break down the action into its component parts. So if you were observing a swimmer, for example, it might be a good idea to break down each different kind of stroke into arm action, leg action, body position, timing and breathing.

Likewise, a lay up shot in basketball could also be broken down into a set of 'mini-skills':

- dribbling
- transfer to two hands
- lay up strides
- jump
- release/placement of shot.

Another very good technique, if you have access to a video camera, is to video the action and then use slow motion and frame-

Technically demanding: for both the performer and the observer!

by-frame replay to give you the time you need to make sure you've observed and noted all the critical areas of the performance.

Another good thing about videoing a performance is that it makes it much easier to analyse your own performance.

Breaking down the action to make observation more focused is a very useful technique. But do remember that you need to build all the components together again for your analysis.

Tactics and team skills

For some activities, particularly games activities, you may be looking for team skills (use of tactics and strategies) as well as individual skills. These can be complicated to observe, so, again, you can break down the action into more manageable areas to focus on. You might, for example, look at defence tactics first, and the type of defensive formation used by one or both teams. You could then observe the attack tactics, and the formations used for attacking in the game.

Roles

If your chosen activity has different roles for participants, you can focus on one role and use the skills that role depends on as the key aspects of your observation. In the case of a goalkeeper, for example, we might observe how well the performer deals with:

- shot stopping
- crosses
- set plays (corners, free kicks and penalties)
- distributing the ball
- decision-making
- fitness
- teamwork/tactics.

Viewpoint

It is important to think about where to observe from – what it the best place to stand to get the best view? In Premier League soccer, some coaches and managers like to watch the game 'pitch-side' from the dug-out, while others prefer the view from the stand. The referee, of course, moves with the action in order to get the best view they can. In tennis, the umpire observes the match from a high viewpoint, and TV coverage of games will often switch viewpoints from above, behind, in front and to the side, or close up on individual performance, or from some distance away, so all the performers can be seen.

For your analysis of performance task, you also need to think about which position or positions is going to give you the best view of the performance. This might change, for example, if you observe one player who is right-handed and one player who is left-handed. It might also change according to weather conditions.

Safety is also a serious consideration for observers as well as for performers and officials. Take care not to position yourself somewhere that could lead to the risk of injury – either to yourself or to others.

Analysis

Analysis of a performance is giving your view on how good it was and where it could be improved. Good analysis depends on your knowing whether the performance you are observing is being done correctly or not.

So how do you go about telling whether a performer is performing a skill correctly or not? A very good way is to use the perfect model technique discussed earlier (page 148), where you have a mental image of how a skill should look when performed correctly. You can then compare this knowledge of how a skill should look with what you are actually observing.

The best way of building up your knowledge of what skills should look like is by watching someone who can do them. This could be your teacher or coach demonstrating them, or top performers in the activity on TV or videos. You will also build up this information from performing these skills yourself.

A good way to observe and analyse skills is to look for the *essential features* and *refining features* of a skill. Kicking a football, for example, is more than just swinging your leg and making contact with the ball: there are a number of different parts to the skill that have to be linked together in order for it to be performed well. The player has to observe the speed and direction of the ball, approach the ball at the correct speed, get their footwork right, time the swing of their leg correctly to hit the ball properly, and follow through the kick. These are all essential features of the skill. If any of these essential features were not performed properly, the kick would be missed or the ball would fly off in the wrong direction. The essential features are crucial for the skill to be performed at all.

The refining features determine how well the skill is performed: the timing of the kick, the angle of contact between the foot and the ball, the force of the kick and how well all the different parts of the skill are linked together.

You can use your knowledge of skills to back up the analysis you make. It is not enough just to state that a particular skill was performed badly or well, you have to explain your reasons. Your explanation should refer to what you know about how a skill or technique *should* have been performed – the perfect model.

Factors affecting performance

The first section in this book looks at a very important part of your GCSE course – factors affecting performance. What makes a performance good or less good is very important for your analysis of performance too. You should be able to demonstrate your knowledge about what might be holding a person's performance back or what is contributing to the excellence of a performance.

You will be able to use the information from the rest of your course to very good effect in the analysis of performance task. Just some of the factors that would be worth bearing in mind when analysing a performance, could include:

- flexibility – was the warm up sufficient for the performance?
- fitness – is the person physically fit enough to perform well?
- mental attitude – is the person motivated or stressed?

Action plan

In your action plan, you can establish:

- particular aspects of the game or individual performance that need to be worked on
- targets or goals for achieving improvement.

Deciding on ways in which a performance can be improved is, like observation and analysis, based on your knowledge about your activity, and your knowledge about the factors affecting performance and about fitness – all of which you will cover in this course.

From your analysis of strengths and weaknesses, you should be able to suggest ways in which the performance can be improved or corrected. For example, you might tell a swimmer to close her fingers together in order to get a better pull, or suggest that she works on her leg kick by pushing a kick board (or float) across the pool.

When you are helping to improve a skill or technique, explaining and demonstrating the perfect model to the performer is usually very productive: perhaps by watching a video of a top performer in action, and then contrasting that with a video of the performer doing the same skill. You should also aim to suggest a training method or methods, or a practice session that could be used to improve performance. By the end of this course, you will have a good knowledge of training methods and practices from your coursework and the work you do in class.

When working out the action plan for your performer (or yourself), you should prioritise which aspects of the performance need to be improved the most. These are the aspects your action plan needs to concentrate on. It's a good idea to set some goals or targets for the improvement of performance. Setting targets for improvement is a good way of motivating people to do the work they need to do in order to improve.

A key part of setting targets is being able to monitor (measure) progress. For example, you might suggest a drill to improve catching in cricket where the performer will aim to catch six balls thrown one after another over a certain distance. If they can consistently catch three balls out of six at the start of the practice session, and five out of six at the end of the session, then you can say that this aspect of performance has been improved.

As part of the analysis of performance task, you will be asked to assess how much improvement there has been in performance as a result of your suggestions after six weeks of practice.

You can use tests to measure improvements in fitness

Feedback

Some people are very good at giving advice, and some people are not as good. Also, some people are very good at taking advice, while some people take advice as criticism. You need to learn the skill of making your feedback clear, so it is easy to understand, and constructive, which means that it is positive.

It is quite difficult to take in lots of information at one time. Try to be selective about your feedback, so you talk about the most important aspects first. Good coaches ask for performers' own opinions on what they think is going well and what not so well, and this is often a good tactic to use.

Most importantly, do remember to talk about the strengths of the performance as well as the weaknesses. No one likes to hear a long list of their faults! On the other hand, people are often much more willing to listen to suggestions about their weaknesses if you have already told them about what they are doing well. Remember also that feedback also refers to the improvement that you hope will result from your suggestions.

Analysis of performance checklist

This is a list of the main things to remember to do in your analysis of performance. Your teacher will give you lots of help in planning your analysis of performance task:

1   Select the activity you want to do your task in. This is most likely to be your strongest activity: the one you know most about.

2   Make a list of the important skills and techniques needed by the player you are going to observe.

3   Observe your chosen player in a role, practice or a game (make sure you record the person's role or position); if you are doing an analysis of yourself, this will probably involve watching a video of yourself.

4   Analyse the performance in order to pick out and describe the strengths.

5   Do the same for the weaknesses of the performance.

6   Suggest ways of improving any strengths or weaknesses.

7   Suggest what training methods or practice sessions could be used to improve performance.

8   After six weeks of practice, assess how much improvement has occurred: make sure you write down your findings.

9   Discuss the results with the player and write down his or her views or reactions (if you've been analysing your own performance, you should discuss your findings with your teacher or coach, and write down their views or reactions).

Tasks

1   Choose *four* different skills from one of your activities and write a description of what you think is the perfect model for each one of those skills.

2   Watch someone from your group perform *one* of these skills. Compare their performance with the perfect model:

   a   Are there any obvious weaknesses compared to the perfect model? Describe what these are.

   b   What are the strengths of their performance? Describe them.

3   Now consider the following questions:

   a   What do you think this person could do to improve their weaknesses and refine their strengths?

   b   Can you suggest any practice or training methods they might use to do this?

Glossary

gliding joint	joint allowing only a small degree of movement of one bone against another, e.g. the carpals	11
glycogen	the form in which the body stores carbohydrate	22
haemoglobin	found in red blood cells and consisting of the protein, globin, and a red- based pigment	28
healthy diet	food intake containing the correct balance and quantity of nutrients	84
hinge joint	joint consisting of one concave bone surface and one convex surface, e.g. the knee joint	10
hyaline cartilage	also called articular cartilage; found on the surface of bones where articulation (see above) occurs	8
interval training	a form of training which alternates periods of exercise and recovery	117
isometric contraction	contraction of the muscle that occurs without any visible movement	120
isotonic contraction	contraction of the muscle involving shortening of the fibres and which produces movement	120
knowledge of performance (KP)	knowledge of a performance received by a performer from an external source	33
knowledge of results (KR)	knowledge about the result of a performance received from an outside source	33
lactic acid	a poison that is a by-product of exercise; causes muscle fatigue, particularly during anaerobic activity	22
ligaments	tough, fibrous tissue that connects one bone to another.	8
mental rehearsal	going over the practising of a skill, or series of skills, in the mind, without any physical movement.	45
motivation (extrinsic)	motivation which is the result of external reward, e.g. cups, medals, prizes or money	46
motivation (intrinsic)	motiviation which is the result of internalised drive, satisfaction or pride, e.g. as a challenge, to keep fit, or for enjoyment	46
muscle atrophy	the wasting of muscle due to prolonged inactivity	125
muscle (cardiac)	muscle found only in the heart	12
muscle hypertrophy	the growth of muscle bulk in response to the demands placed upon it	74
muscle (involuntary)	smooth muscle controlling internal organs, over which we have no conscious control	12
muscle (skeletal or voluntary)	striped or striated muscle over which we do have conscious control	12
muscle insertion	the point at which a muscle is attached to the bone it is effective in moving	12
muscle origin	the point at which a muscle is attached to the bone against which movement is produced	12
network centres	e.g National Network Centres; part of the network of élite performance centres developed by Sport England (see below)	71
open skills	skills that are performed in an unstable, changing environment and which are subject to change, e.g. kicking a football	34
overload	the increasing of a workload forcing muscles to adapt to new demands	108
oxygen debt	the volume of oxygen consumed during recovery from exercise in excess of that which would normally be consumed in the same period	22
part learning	the learning of a skill in small parts or sub-routines	38

perfect model	an ideal performance of a skill on which learning can be based	148
performance enhancing drugs	substances (usually banned) which artificially improve performance	95
pivot joint	joint formed by two bones, one consisting of a peg and the other a receptive ring, e.g. the atlas and axis bone (head and neck)	11
prime mover	the muscle which instigates or initiates movement	12
process goals	goals or targets based on improving skills or tactics	49
processing information	the receiving and processing of data leading to the production of a physical skill	35
progression	an extension of overload (see above) which reflects the progressive increase in an aspect of fitness, e.g. strength	109
red blood cells	cells that carry oxygen to where it is needed in the body	28
respiratory system	the organs of the body involved in the inhalation and expiration of air	20
RICE	First-aid procedure; an acronym for: **R**est **I**ce **C**ompression **E**levation	143
safe training zone	the safe limit of pulse rate during aerobic training, e.g. 60-85 per cent of maximum heart rate depending on age [The Karvonen Principle]	113
sit and reach test	used to assess flexibility in the hamstrings and lower back	107
skill-related fitness	those elements of fitness involved in the performance of skill, e.g. agility, balance, limb speeda	80
somatotype	a method of classifying body shape: ectomorph – thin; mesomorph – muscular; endomorph – fat or rounded	86
specificity	the relevance and appropriateness of training for a particular sport or activity	108
Sport England	The senior sports body in England (not UK)	70
stress	state of tension caused by the lack of ability, or the perceived lack of ability, to perform a task	96
stroke volume	the volume of blood pumped from the left vetricle of the heart in one beat	24
synergist	a muscle which contracts in order to assist the prime mover (see above), e.g. the deltoids often assist the biceps by stabilising the shoulder joint	12
synovial joint	allows the widest range of movement and is contained within a joint capsule (synovial capsule)	8
target goals	or outcome goals; aimed at improving results or outcomes, e.g. a new personal best	49
tendons	connective tissue that attaches muscle to bone. Not to be confused with ligaments	8
tendon of insertion	the tendon attaching a muscle to the bone being moved	18
tendon of origin	the tendon attaching a muscle to the bone against which movement is obtained.	18
tidal volume	the volume of air inhaled or exhaled in one breath	27
twelve-minute run	also known as the Cooper twelve-minute run. Distance measured after 12 minutes – used as an indication of aerobic endurance	100
UKSI	The United Kingdom Sports Institute	71
UK Sport	The United Kingdom Sports Council	71
verruca	a wart found on the foot; also known as plantar wart	139
vital capacity	the total volume of air that can be moved in and out of the lungs in one breath	27
VO_2 max	the maximum amount of oxygen used in one minute per kilogram of bodyweight	98
white blood cells	transparent cells that digest bacteria and fight infection	29
whole learning	the learning of a skill or series of skills as a complete routine	38